Old Master Drawings

Old Master Drawings

from the
Ashmolean Museum

Christopher White
Catherine Whistler
Colin Harrison

Ashmolean Museum Oxford
in association with Oxford University Press
1992

This exhibition was originally shown in Rome, at the
Palazzo Ruspoli, from 13 May to 13 July 1991 and
subsequently in Oxford from 18 August to 11 October 1992,
as part of the European Arts Festival

Text and illustrations:
(c) The University of Oxford: Ashmolean Museum, Oxford
1991

British Library Cataloguing in Publication Data

White, Christopher
        Old Master Drawings from the Ashmolean Museum,
        Oxford
        I. Title
        741.9

ISBN 1-85444-020-9 (paperback)
ISBN 1-85444-027-6 (case bound)

Cover illustration: Raphael, Portrait of the Artist, no. 11

Text layout and cover design by Cole design unit, Reading
Text set in Apollo by Meridian Phototypesetting Limited,
Pangbourne-on-Thames
Colour origination by Leonardo-De Luca Editori, Italy
Printed and bound in Great Britain by Jolly & Barber Limited,
Rugby 1992

Contents

To the memory of James Byam Shaw CBE (1903–1992), long-time friend and benefactor of the Ashmolean Print Room

This catalogue was printed with generous grants from the European Arts Festival and from Katrin Bellinger

Foreword

The exhibition of one hundred Old Master drawings from the Museum's collection is being held as part of the European Arts Festival to celebrate Britain's Presidency of the European Community. The selection of drawings was made on the occasion of the exhibition held during 1991 in the Palazzo Ruspoli, Rome, which was generously sponsored by the Fondazione Memmo. In order to produce an English version of the catalogue, which was originally published by Leonardo-De Luca, we are greatly indebted to Mr John Drummond of the European Arts Festival and to Miss Katrin Bellinger.

Within the Museum the photography was handled most expertly by Mrs Vera Magyar and Mr Michael Dudley and his colleagues in the photographic department. The entries were written by Dr Catherine Whistler (nos. 1–44), Mr Colin Harrison (nos. 75–86), who also served as a most efficient research assistant, and myself (nos. 45–74 and 87–100). The authors would like to acknowledge with gratitude the basic research on the drawings carried out by former colleagues in the Museum.

Christopher White
Director

Introduction

History of the Museum

The Ashmolean Museum, which today contains the major part of the University's collections of art and archaeology, was founded as a result of the offer made by Elias Ashmole in 1677 to give Oxford the 'closet of rarities' formerly belonging to the elder and the younger John Tradescant, augmented with coins, medals and manuscripts from his own collection.

Sir Thomas Bodley had already in his Library, which was opened in 1602, provided a gallery for objects of antiquity or curiosity belonging to the University, and nearby were placed the ancient marbles bequeathed in 1654 by the antiquary, John Selden, and the Earl of Arundel's collection of marble inscriptions given by his grandson, Lord Henry Howard, in 1667.

In making his offer Ashmole had stipulated that a suitable building should be constructed to house the collections, along with a lecture theatre and a 'chemical laboratory', and at considerable cost to the University this was carried out most handsomely by Thomas Wood on a site next to the Sheldonian Theatre. When it was opened in 1683 by the Duke and Duchess of York with an inspection of the 'rarities', a lavish banquet and some scientific experiments, it became the first institutional museum in Britain and arguably throughout Europe.

The Tradescants, gardeners to Charles I amongst others, had assembled from all over the world a collection, which became known internationally as 'The Ark', comprising natural history, medical and ethnographical specimens, as well as paintings, coins and antiquities. When the Ashmolean opened it was established as the centre of scientific studies in the University for over two hundred years as well as a place for the display of the University's treasures. To the founding collection were soon added new and important accessions, which included such famous objects as the Alfred Jewel, presented to the University in 1718.

In the later eighteenth century the University collections were sadly neglected. To provide a more suitable place for the display of antique sculpture, which by then included the celebrated 'Arundel Marbles', the remnants of the Earl's collection of statuary formed in the early seventeenth century, benefactions were made by the Revd Dr Francis Randolph and Sir Roger Newdigate. This money eventually allowed the construction of a new building in Beaumont Street designed by Charles Robert Cockerell, which is is one of the finest examples of neo-Grecian architecture in Britain. The new University

Galleries, as they were called, were opened in 1845 with the antique sculpture from the Arundel collection displayed in the Randolph Gallery on the ground floor, and the pictures transferred from the Bodleian and elsewhere on the first floor.

The opening of the new galleries had the immediate effect of attracting important gifts to the University. Apart from various collections of drawings which will be mentioned below, the Fox-Strangways gift in 1850 of forty early Italian paintings, including Uccello's masterpiece of a *Hunt in the Forest*, the Chambers Hall gift of Old Master paintings as well as drawings in 1855, John Ruskin's deposit of thirty six watercolours by J.M.W. Turner in 1881 and Pre-Raphaelite paintings belonging to Thomas Combe in 1894, all added greatly to the representation of Western art in the collection.

In the meantime the rapidly expanding collections housed in the old Ashmolean building made a more logical distribution of the objects throughout the University inevitable, an action which also reflected the rationalisation of academic disciplines in general. The coins and medals were transferred to the Bodleian coin cabinet, the natural history sections to the University Museum (opened in 1860) and the ethnographical exhibits to the Pitt Rivers Museum (founded in 1886). What was left in the old Ashmolean was largely archaeological, and with the arrival of the first of what were to be a long series of acquisitions from excavations in Egypt, starting with those made by Sir Flinders Petrie, all available space was soon exhausted.

Thanks to the generosity of the distinguished collector, C.D.E.Fortnum, acting on the initiative of the then Keeper of the Ashmolean, Sir Arthur Evans, a large extension to the Beaumont Street building was added in 1894. This enabled the transfer of the remaining collections in the old Ashmolean to the new building, and led in 1908 to the formal unification of the two institutions as the Ashmolean Museum of Art and Archaeology operating as a single administrative body with two departments, Antiquities and Fine Art (later to become Western Art).

During this century the collections have grown immeasurably, primarily from the gift or bequest of specialised collections, such as those made by John Evans of prehistoric antiquities, Sir John Beazley of Greek and Etruscan vases, the Hill family of musical instruments, Daisy Linda Ward of Dutch and Flemish still-life paintings, John Francis Mallett of oriental porcelain, ivories, Limoges enamels and European clocks and watches, and Mr and Mrs H.R.Marshall of Worcester porcelain, as well as a number of other important collections. The Department of Antiquities was enriched by the deposit of objects from archaeological excavations made, for example, by Arthur Evans at Knossos and Professor F.H.Griffiths in Nubia.

In 1922 the Heberden Coin Room opened, bringing together many of the collections spread throughout the University including those of the Bodleian and some of the colleges and going back in time to the collections of coins assembled by Archbishop Laud, the Tradescants and Ashmole in the early seventeenth century. The Department of Eastern Art was founded in 1962 with the transfer of the oriental collections from the Indian Institute, some of which, such as the Sayce, Farrer and Mallett collections of oriental porcelain, were previously in Beaumont Street. Within thirty years the collection has been transformed by outstanding gifts and bequests made by such distinguished collectors as Sir Herbert Ingram (Chinese ceramics and bronzes), Sir Alan Barlow (Islamic pottery), Eric North (Chinese lacquer) and Gerald Reitlinger (Chinese, Japanese and Islamic ceramics).

With the Cast Gallery, which contains a very fine collection of classical casts, the Museum now houses five departments. Like its counterpart in Cambridge, the Fitzwilliam Museum, the collections of which it so nicely complements, the Ashmolean ranks as a museum of international stature second only in importance in Britain to the great national collections.

History of the collecting of Old Master drawings from the Renaissance to the late eighteenth century in the Ashmolean Museum[1]

The opening of the new building in Beaumont Street in 1845 was celebrated by one of the most outstanding gifts it has been the privilege of any museum to receive, namely some 270 drawings by or attributed to Raphael and Michelangelo formerly belonging to Sir Thomas Lawrence, who had died in 1830. This gift immediately gave the Ashmolean what has remained the finest collection of drawings by Raphael in the world and one of the three finest assemblies of drawings by Michelangelo. But if the gift to Oxford represents a glorious end to the dispersal of part of the Lawrence collection, the earlier parts of the story must represent one of the least creditable sagas regarding the arts in Britain.

---

[1] For a fuller account see the introductions to Parker I and II, Macandrew and Brown (1982), as well as Sutton, pp. vii–xxxiii, for the dispersal of the Lawrence collection. By omitting the nineteenth and twentieth centuries from the scope of the exhibition, a number of gifts and bequests are not discussed.

During his life Lawrence had amassed one of the finest if not the finest collection of Old Master drawings in the history of collecting. It is probably true to say that if Charles I's collection of paintings and Lawrence's collection of drawings remained intact today Britain would hold Renaissance and Baroque paintings and drawings unrivalled in quality by any other country in the world. Lawrence's collection was outstanding for the substantial groups of works by Leonardo, Dürer, Parmigianino, Rembrandt, Rubens, Van Dyck, Claude, the Carracci amongst others, as well as, above all, the incomparable series of drawings by Raphael and Michelangelo. (Raphael was Lawrence's favourite artist, whom he considered 'not only the Phenomenon but the Philosopher of his art, and his judgement was even greater than his genius'.) Aware of its great importance and keen to preserve it intact for the nation, his will stipulated that before it could be dispersed it should be offered for £18,000, which represented under half of the sum of upward of £40,000 he had disbursed, to four nominees to be approached in the following order: King George IV, the Trustees of the British Museum, Sir Robert Peel, the statesman and collector of paintings (many of which were later bought by the National Gallery) and Lord Dudley, a patron revered by Lawrence. If unsold within two years the collection was to be put up for public auction.

That Lawrence's public spirited offer was met with nothing but apathy is a tragedy for this country. The King was ailing and was to die later in the year. The Trustees of the British Museum showed little awareness of the importance of the drawings and made no attempt to try and raise the money. And neither Peel nor Dudley were interested. Only the Royal Academy, which voted a contribution of £1,000 towards the purchase, thanks primarily to the support of its President, Sir Martin Archer Shee, emerges with honour. The government like many of its successors was indifferent to promoting the arts, and from a political point of view was more concerned with the social unrest in the country during the post-Napoleonic era. Although some half-hearted attempts were made in favour of the collection's acquisition, the members of the government, as the *Spectator* reported, 'haggled out and chaffered in a huckstering spirit that any mere trader would have been ashamed at'. It was left to a foreigner to make the most succinct comment about the whole affair. After having an opportunity to see the collection Prince Talleyrand remarked: 'si vous n'achetez pas ces choses-là, vous êtes des barbares'.

In 1834, faced with such indifference, Lawrence's executor disposed of the whole collection to Samuel Woodburn, the dealer who had played a prime role in its formation and who was no less determined to save it for the nation. After various abortive attempts Woodburn arranged a series of ten short exhibitions with the final two assigned to the drawings of Raphael and Michelangelo. Despite some interest and interminable haggling over price, no purchaser for either of the last two sales emerged and under apparent royal pressure Woodburn agreed to sell a group by both artists to the Prince of Orange, later King William II of Holland. (The latter's collection was later to be sold and a number of drawings returned to Britain.) To compensate for the losses from the collection, Woodburn purchased the collection of Jeremiah Harman, but apart from two superb Raphaels (no. 11) this was a totally inadequate replacement.

It was only in 1841, three years after negotiations with the government had finally broken down, that the scene of activity in the campaign to save the Raphael and Michelangelo drawings moved from London to Oxford. The prime mover was the Revd Dr Henry Wellesley, who was a distinguished collector of drawings himself. A graduate of the University, and a kinsman to its Chancellor, the Duke of Wellington, he returned to Oxford as Vice-Principal of New Inn Hall in 1842, later becoming Principal. After seeing the drawings on show at Woodburn's gallery prior to being sent abroad, Wellesley, still a country clergyman in Sussex, wrote to the then Principal of New Inn Hall: 'They are wonderful! And I could not help thinking of your past observations respecting the new Galleries at Oxford; Fine Paintings we shall never be able to get, but a selection of genuine old drawings we might very well hope to obtain. Now here is an opportunity, such as never can occur again, of forming at once a Gallery which even without further delay will never be surpassed . . . these two Masters once secured, the difficulty is over: second-rate drawings are always to be purchased, and if not purchased or presented are not much to be regretted. . . . No time should be lost if this grand project is to be secured for Alma Mater'.

It was a clever move to associate the possible acquisition of the drawings with the projected opening of the new museum building, and attracted considerable support from a number of influential figures within the University. C.R.Cockerell, who described himself 'as the workman engaged to build a receptacle for such precious remains', offered his support. But, for anyone aware of the history of the University, for every protagonist can be found an opponent, and a group of the latter fought a vigorous and even malicious campaign, imputing financial gain rather than public-spiritedness to Woodburn in offering the drawings to Oxford for the very reasonable sum of £10,000. (According to Woodburn these drawings cost Lawrence above £30,000). After the inevitable numerous and lengthy debates that any move in favour of positive action engenders within the University, it was eventually agreed in November 1841 to form an official committee to sponsor an appeal for subscriptions. Supporters in favour of the drawings within the University claimed variously that their acquisition would improve the artistic taste of the students as well as of design in general, promote morality and possibly inspire an artistic Renaissance in Britain.

The campaign started well and about a third of the amount required was raised. But at that point it moved into the doldrums and it must have seemed that a general project to save the Lawrence collection, which had begun over a decade earlier, was no nearer a happy solution even to one albeit important part. The problem was, as Woodburn said on an earlier occasion, the old story of 'plenty of good wishes and promises but no active or true assistance'. In desperation, Woodburn, who was being actively approached by would-be Continental purchasers, made a number of proposals such as an offer to exhibit the drawings in Oxford, or to sell the Michelangelo drawings separately. Or even, how little did he know the University, that the latter might make a subscription. But for one reason or another none met with favour. It was then at the eleventh hour that help came from a totally unexpected source. The second Earl of Eldon, a graduate of the University, whose name had not previously been mentioned in connexion with the Lawrence collection, came forward with an offer of £3,000. Woodburn, impressed by the largest act of generosity since the whole affair had begun in 1830, reduced his asking price by a similar sum. Eldon thereupon increased his subscription by another £1,000 and the successful outcome of the appeal was virtually assured. In the long and at times painful saga, there were three heroes: Samuel Woodburn, for his seemingly inexhaustible patience, the Reverend Henry Wellesley as the prime mover, and the Earl of Eldon for his magnificent generosity. In July 1845 twenty cases containing the drawings were delivered to the University Galleries in Beaumont Street.

Encouraged by this success Woodburn hoped that other parts of the Lawrence collection might be purchased by other benefactors for Oxford. He at first offered the group of drawings by Parmigianino and when these were sold he proposed 'the superb Collection of early Italian and German drawings prior to the time of Raffaelle for Italy and A. Dürer for Germany'. But if he was disappointed, other drawings once belonging to Lawrence have from time to time, even as recently as thirty years ago, entered the collection. The most substantial addition was the group of some forty drawings by or attributed to the Carracci presented in 1853 by the first Earl of Ellesmere. These were selected from the entire series of over 150 drawings by those artists in Woodburn's sixth exhibition in 1836, which the Earl bought shortly afterwards. But it has to be admitted that apart from a few exceptional drawings (see no. 25) Ellesmere kept the best of the drawings for himself. These remained in the family's succession until they were sold by the sixth Duke of Sutherland at auction in 1972, when the Museum acquired two (no. 26).

In 1850 the Delegates of the Clarendon Press, possibly influenced by the Raphael/Michelangelo gift, transferred an outstanding group of English watercolours for the *Oxford Almanack*, which since 1768 had been illustrated with topographical views of Oxford by various artists including Edward Dayes and in 1799 and for some years thereafter the young J.M.W.Turner.

In 1855 another gift came to the Museum which was a worthy complement to the Raphael/Michelangelo series of nine years earlier. Chambers Hall, who was born in 1786 and died in 1855, was a somewhat mysterious figure, who lived with his brother at first in Southampton and later in London – it was in the latter city that Dr Waagen inspected his collection. Like his brother he was a competent watercolourist, making expeditions to the Continent, but otherwise little is known about him apart from his collecting activities. As Sir Karl Parker observed, 'For absolute purity, the Chambers Hall benefaction is second to no other component part of the collection . . . its donor stands forth as a connoisseur of impeccable taste and almost unerring judgement'. Apart from a gift to the British Museum, which included an outstanding group of works by Thomas Girtin, the main beneficiary of his great generosity was the Ashmolean Museum. In addition to paintings, numbering, for example, ten out of the eleven accepted Rubens sketches now in the collection, as well as works by Van Dyck, Guardi and Constable, and a group of prints of the finest quality, he gave a remarkable series of drawings demonstrating his width of taste in his selection of artists. From the time of the Renaissance are drawings by Dürer, Leonardo (nos. 3–4), both from the Lawrence collection, Raphael and Correggio; from the seventeenth century are sheets by Rubens (nos. 57 and 59), Rembrandt (no. 62) and Claude (no. 75); and from the eighteenth century examples by Canaletto, Guardi and Richard Wilson. Although by no means eschewing figure drawings, as can be seen from the list of artists just mentioned, he showed a predilection for landscapes, reflecting his own artistic interests.

There are no records of his collecting activities, although he was generally recognised for his distinction in this field. From correspondence with the Reverend Henry Wellesley, who may well have played a decisive role, he appears to have intended his gift to the University for a long period of time, referring to its fulfilment as 'a long cherished desire'. On the occasion it was made in the year of his death, the *Oxford Journal* describes him as 'well known for his refined taste and judgement in subjects connected with the arts of design'.

While Chambers Hall was outstanding for his sense of quality, Francis Douce was notable for his antiquarianism, which affected both his career and his collecting. Born in London in 1757, a generation earlier than Chambers Hall, he took up a legal career which he then abandoned for scholarship. A period as Keeper of Manuscripts at the British Museum was terminated as a result of friction between himself and the Trustees. It was reported that the polite welcome he received on a visit to Oxford in 1830 led to his decision to bequeath to the University his vast collection, which included books, manuscripts, coins and prints as well as drawings. When the collection was received after his death in 1834 it was housed in the Bodleian and it took nearly thirty years before the Curators of the Library agreed to transfer the prints and drawings to the Ashmolean, where the drawings still remain the largest individual part of the collection.

A certain capriciousness and eccentricity in his character is also reflected in his collecting. Antiquarian interest and taste for curiosities rather than aesthetic beauty determined what he acquired. Although owning some Italian drawings (for example, nos. 19, 32 and 34), the principal riches of his collection belong to the early German (nos. 67–73 and 87) and the Netherlandish schools (nos. 45, 49, 52–53 and 55), including outstanding studies by Hans Holbein the Younger (no. 87) and Altdorfer (no. 70). The undisputed masterpiece belonging to Douce, which remains one of the principal treasures of the Museum, was what still is the only drawing by Grünewald (no. 69) in a British collection. But as Sir Karl Parker observed, 'Churlish as the suggestion may seem, it had almost certainly in Douce's eyes the interest of age and oddity rather than the irresistible appeal of a work of genius'. The addition of his English drawings of the Stuart period has given the Museum the second largest holding after the British Museum. Douce's collection also contained two large groups of drawings by British artists. Traditionally the Rowlandsons (no. 99) are said to have been purchased directly from the artist. He was certainly a friend of John Flaxman (see no. 98), acting as one of his executors, and his acquisitions of drawings from the artist or from his estate has given the Ashmolean the largest holding in a public collection.

In this century the gifts and bequests to the Museum have continued but individually have tended to be smaller in number. The collection of exceptionally good British watercolours belonging to Professor Francis Pierrepont Barnard, some of which were given in 1916 and others bequeathed in 1934, included the two very fine watercolours by John Robert Cozens shown here (nos. 96–97). Mrs Florence Weldon's generosity to the Museum began with her first gift in 1915 and continued until her bequest in 1937. Best known for the very heterogeneous group of paintings she acquired for or gave to the Ashmolean, which includes Claude's last dated work, *Ascanius shooting the Stag of Sylvia*, she also donated some drawings, which apart from contemporary works included one of Claude's preparatory drawings (no. 76) for the Ashmolean painting, as well as a Gainsborough (no. 91). The tradition is that she would appear in the Museum unannounced bearing a work of art wrapped in brown paper, which she would leave at the bookstall with the words, 'This is for the Keeper'.

In 1934 Sir Karl Parker was appointed Keeper of the Department of Fine Art, as it was then known, and there began one of the most remarkable periods of acquisitions of drawings in the Museum's history. In an early annual report he wrote that one of his principal aims was 'to extend and develop' the collection of drawings and he nobly fulfilled his promise so that by the time he retired in 1962 he had added well over 3,000 drawings representing all schools to the collection. In 1934, for example, no less than 236 drawings were acquired, and in 1950, 210. And over one third of the present selection is made up of drawings added to the collection during Parker's Keepership. With his combination of taste and knowledge, he was the right man at the right time. The period from the time he became Keeper until after the Second World War was not a prosperous time for art dealers and an active collector even with only modest funds at his disposal was able to make remarkable purchases. He was assiduous in visiting art dealers, with whom he maintained the kind of friendly relations which encouraged them to give the first offer of a fine or unusual drawing to the Museum. Above all his longtime friend, Dr James Byam Shaw of Colnaghi's, a scholar of no lesser distinction, can be given credit for putting many fine drawings in Parker's way. The latter brought to his acquisition policy a systematic approach with the stated purpose of building up a comprehensive holding of drawings, irrespective of fashion, from the early Renaissance up to and including the present century. In addition to the fine examples by the great masters, such as Bellini (no. 1), Parmigianino (no. 18), from the Lawrence collection, Bernini (no. 31), Guardi (no. 40), Lucas van Leyden (no. 46), Rubens (no. 58), Rembrandt (no. 61) and Dürer (no. 66), he acquired a host of drawings by lesser artists, often of exceptional quality, such as the Annibale Carracci (no. 27), the Jan Brueghel (no. 54) and the Lely (no. 88). And he was himself a generous donor to the Museum, presenting, for example, the Watteau (no. 79), an artist on whom he became the leading authority, and the Hubert Robert (no. 84). But if only an inveterate optimist would expect to encounter another such golden age of acquisitions, it can be claimed that Parker on his retirement left the Ashmolean in the position of being one of the great print rooms of the world, second in importance in this country only to the British Museum.

Christopher White

Acknowledgements

The authors would like thank the following for help with individual entries: Brigid Cleaver, David Ekserdjian, Sir Brinsley Ford, Paul Joannides, Nicholas Purcell, Clare Robertson, Jeremy Rex-Parkes, Kate de Rothschild, Richard Rutherford, Rick Scorza, Aidan Weston-Lewis, and Jon Whiteley.

(?) Giovanni Bellini

(b. Venice/Padua *c.* 1435; d. Venice 1516)

1 Studies for a recumbent Figure of the Infant Christ

Brush drawing in brown, washed and heightened with body-colour. 206 × 285.

Verso: A Female Martyr

Pen and ink with brown wash, heightened with body-colour and squared for enlargement in black chalk.

Collections:
>Jonathan Richardson, Junior (L. 2170); Earl of Dalhousie; Mrs Broun Lindsay. Purchased in 1939.

Selected literature:
>Byam Shaw (1935); Parker, II, no. 2; Parker (1958), no. 3; Lauts, no. 40; Heinemann, no. V316; Robertson, pp. 48–49; Pignatti (1977), no. 9; Muraro, no. C501.

Bellini's name has been associated with this appealing but enigmatic drawing since it was first published by Byam Shaw. The technique is a familiar one in Venetian late Quattrocento drawings: the blue paper (first popularized by Venetian artists) provides a cool middle tone for a very controlled drawing in which a fine brush is dipped in ink and wash for the contours and shadows, and white pigment is added for the highlighting of the flesh and drapery. The technique was one used notably by Carpaccio for head and figure studies (see no. 5); rarer examples of such highly finished preparatory drawings by Cima da Conegliano,[1] or Giovanni Bellini have come down to us.[2]

A connexion can be made between this drawing and a painting of the 1480s from Bellini's workshop, the *Winthrop Madonna*, now in the Harvard University Art Museum.[3] At first glance the figure of the Christ Child in the picture is very similar. However, the Child is altogether a plumper and sweeter figure there, unlike the stiff, intense baby of the drawing. Further, the Child in the painting is shown with curly hair, a plain sash, and with His right hand on His breast. As Byam Shaw pointed out, the drawing is undoubtedly of higher quality than the painting, which is a derivation from a prototype by the master.

The drawing is a very beautiful and skilful one; however, some elements suggest that it is a workshop drawing, based on a design by Giovanni Bellini. Thus, the modelling of the right leg and foot is a little clumsy, and the head is not set very happily on the shoulders (in fact, the shadowing behind cuts in too deeply at the neck). The draughtsman was keen to perfect the figure, and made corrections to the outline of the head and chest with a blue water-colour; the same blue was used to heighten some of the meticulous shadowing on the face. This suggests that the artist was attempting to copy accurately, or work up successfully in his master's manner, a design by Bellini, even down to the placing of the separate studies of the Infant's legs on the sheet. Although there is scant evidence for this kind of drawing practice in Bellini's workshop, the drawing has the characteristics of a copy by a very good hand, perhaps even made from a life drawing by the master. The drawing's beauty is, of course, the principal argument for the authorship of Bellini himself.

The polished, crisp quality of this finished drawing, and its hardness of detail (the head looks almost as thought it has been carved out of wood), suggest two possibilities. Bellini's prototype could have shared those qualities, in which case the original drawing must have been an early one, when Paduan influences were dominant. Robertson judged it to reflect Bellini's style of the late 1460s, and attributed it to a close associate of the master at that time, Lauro Padovano (fl. 1470–1500), whom he considers to be the author of the *St Vincent Ferrer Polyptych* of *c.* 1470. On the other hand, the master's design could display the imprint of a new hand in this study, and thus the authorship of the young Carpaccio in the late 1480s has been proposed by Lauts (although Muraro, probably rightly, sees no connexion with Carpaccio). Other names proposed include Cima da Conegliano (whose earlier paintings reveal the same cool, sculptural effects) by Pignatti, and Benedetto Montagna by Heinemann. Bellini ran a busy workshop, and had numerous followers. A good deal of his production of popular devotional pictures was

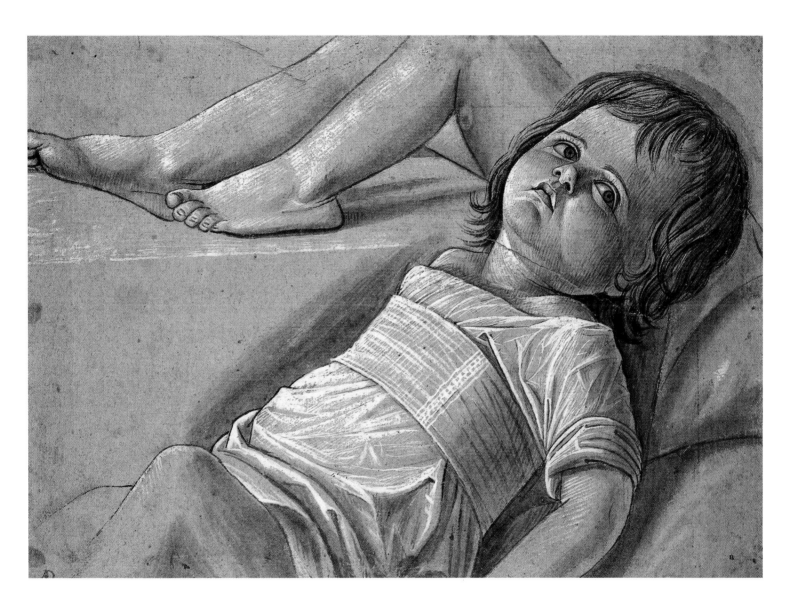

carried out by assistants, who had to be trained in the master's style. It seems best to view the Ashmolean work against this background as a *simile* drawing, depicting one of a stock of motifs invented by the master.

The *verso* is rather different in feel: here, there is a study for the figure of a female martyr, holding a palm. The medium is the same, but the drawing has a very different function as a working drawing squared up for enlargement, hence it is more freely handled and less finished. The figure is seen from a low viewpoint, with the light falling from the left, and the face is somewhat schematically indicated. The roughly sketched black chalk head on the right seems to be by a later hand, and may be unconnected. It may, however, be simply a rough underdrawing: the long hair and band around the head suggest that it is an interpretation of the drawing on the left (the head viewed from another angle?). Again, some names have been proposed for the author of this sensitive study, from Alvise Vivarini[4] to perhaps Bartolommeo Montagna (Heinemann), to the possibility of Benedetto Carpaccio (Muraro). Some shared characteristics with Bellini's early drawings can be discerned, however, such as the schematic treatment of the eyes and nose. The treatment of drapery, with close attention to the crinkles and folds, together with the sensitive, long-fingered hands, are comparable with two drawings of Apostles in the Musée Bonnat, Bayonne.[5] The study could be for the figure of an attendant saint in an altar-piece.[6] Bellini generally made pen and ink studies for such figures; however, this study is one of light and shade, and of volume, for which the three tone technique is appropriate.

It is difficult to judge whether the drawings on recto and verso are by the same hand, given their opposite purposes - the one a carefully finished and corrected image, the other a functional working drawing. However, both in different ways have striking affinities with the work of Giovanni Bellini, and the association with his name must be retained, although the question of authorship has not been resolved.

1 Verso. G.Bellini (?), *A Female Martyr*

[1] British Museum, London; Popham & Pouncey, no. 40.
[2] Royal Collection, Windsor; Popham & Wilde, no. 2*.
[3] Heinemann, no. 27, fig. 55.
[4] Pignatti (1963), p. 48.
[5] Bean, nos. 10 and 11, datable around 1474.
[6] Parker reported Goldscheider's suggestion that the drawing was by Martino da Udine, with the standing saint preparatory for a figure in the Brera *St Ursula and her attendants* dated 1507. However, Tempestini, no. 23, gives this picture to Giovanni Martini. The connexion with the drawing seems slight.

Pietro Vannucci, called Perugino

(b. Castello della Pieve 1466/67; d. Fontignano 1523)

2 Studies for Tobias and the Angel

Silver-point, heightened with body-colour (oxidized) on a pale creamy preparation.
238 × 283.

Collections:
J.-B.-J. Wicar; Sir Thomas Lawrence (L. 2445); Samuel Woodburn. Presented in 1846.

Selected literature:
Fischel (1917), no. 56; Parker, II, no. 27; Scarpellini, under no. 105.

Perugino studied these figures from the life in preparation for a polyptych of *c.* 1496, commissioned by Lodovico il Moro for the Certosa at Pavia. The altar-piece took some time to produce, for the commission had not been completed by 1499. Three panels from the polyptych are now in the National Gallery, London: the central panel of the *Virgin and Child with an Angel,* and the flanking left and right hand panels of *St Michael* and *St Raphael with the young Tobias* (a popular subject, from the apocryphal Book of Tobit).[1]

The positions of Tobias and the Archangel in the final picture are very similar to those taken up by the *garzoni* (studio apprentices) in this drawing. Indeed, the detail of the fish, suspended from a thin cord around Tobias's wrist, is already indicated in the drawing. Perugino was particularly concerned with the expressive function of heads and hands here: the boy's head is studied separately in two drawings on the left, while the delicate linking of the hands of the protagonists and the Archangel's hand carrying the little casket (with the entrails of the fish) are also closely examined in separate studies. These details are central to the narrative. Although this is a life drawing, Perugino in fact set down, with the precise, stiff medium of silver-point, a carefully distilled image. Two rhythmic and elegant forms result, not from the artist's anatomical study or observation, but from a characteristic process of abstraction.

---

[1] Davies, pp. 403–07, no. 288.

Leonardo da Vinci

(b. Anchiano 1452; d. Clos-Lucé 1519)

3   A Maiden with a Unicorn

Pen and dark brown ink, with traces of preliminary indentations with the stylus. 95 × 75.

Collections:

Sir Thomas Lawrence (L. 2445); Samuel Woodburn; Chambers Hall (L. 551), by whom presented in 1855.

Selected literature:

Popham (1946), no. 28B; Parker, II, no. 15; Sutton, no. 5; Kemp, no. 80.

This charming composition illustrates in microcosm Leonardo's poetic invention, and his perennial interest in allegory and emblem. According to legend, only a virgin could tame a unicorn; the animal is therefore associated with love and chastity, and this little scene can be interpreted as an Allegory of Chastity. It is an early example of Leonardo's interest in small scale, sometimes elaborate, compositions in which a human figure is set in relation to animals whose actions are charged with symbolical meanings.[1] The drawing can also be viewed in the context of courtly portraiture, where an animal is included so as to provide an insight into the personality of the sitter, as in Leonardo's *Lady with an Ermine* of *c.* 1485, now in Cracow. This drawing is not, however, a portrait but rather an invention, a *concetto*, which the artist may not have intended to take any further.

Leonardo explored the idea of a composition showing a young girl with a unicorn in another sheet in the British Museum,[2] which was probably preliminary to this one. There, he first made a sketch in lead-point showing the unicorn seated in front of the girl, on her right, gazing up at her; he then quickly re-drew the scene above, with lead-point and pen and ink, with the unicorn now on the girl's left, again at her feet and seen in profile with its head directly above her lap. Leonardo drew framing lines around this very sketchy composition to establish its final shape. The Ashmolean drawing represents a further development, in that the unicorn has now been moved to a position just behind the girl, whom we now see in full view, and who points to the beast, as in the other two sketches, but also clearly holds its reins. The unicorn is in a challenging foreshortened pose, facing the spectator rather than the girl, but with his horn pointing towards her, returning her gesture.

The British Museum sketches are on the verso of a sheet of studies of *The Virgin and Child with a Cat*, part of a group of drawings which were thought to date from *c.* 1478, but which possibly date from a little later, *c.* 1481.[3] The unicorn sketches were undoubtedly made at the same time. An engraving by Agostino Veneziano of 1516 substantially reproduces, in reverse, the composition of the Ashmolean drawing.[4]

[1] Musée du Louvre, Paris and Metropolitan Museum of Art, New York; Popham (1946), nos. 110A and 111.
[2] Popham (1946), no. 27; Popham & Pouncey, no. 98 *verso*.
[3] See Turner, under no. 4.
[4] Bartsch, XIV, p. 288, no. 379.

4   A Unicorn dipping its Horn into a Pool of Water

Pen and ink with metal-point. 94 × 81.

Collections:
     Sir Thomas Lawrence (L. 2445); Samuel Woodburn; Chambers Hall (L. 551), by whom presented in 1855.

Selected literature:
     Popham (1946), no. 60A; Parker, II, no. 16; Sutton, no. 6; Kemp, no. 81.

Leonardo's interest in unicorns and other fabulous animals was fed by his reading of Pliny's *Historia Naturalis* and of the Greek Physiologus, a collection of moralizing and symbolical tales from natural history which was known in the late fourth century, translated into Latin soon afterwards, and subsequently into the vernacular. These sources provided material for mediaeval bestiaries. Many traditional symbols with a religious connotation, such as the Pelican, the Phoenix and the Unicorn, owe their origin to the commentaries of early Christian writers on the *Physiologus*, and were taken up in Romanesque and Gothic church decoration, and in other types of mediaeval art.

     In a religious context, the unicorn was often associated with the Incarnation of Christ, just as the virgin who tames it was identified with the Virgin Mary. Among the legends accruing to this emblematic animal was that of its power to purify poisoned water by making the sign of the Cross with its horn, which is the scene depicted here. The unicorn is drawn with marvellous vigour and economy, in a complex pose with the form dramatically silhouetted — a type of drawing Leonardo made at different times in his career, as in some later sheets of animal studies.[1] A fragment of another study of a unicorn or a horse, moving to the right, is drawn in lead-point on the same sheet.

---

[1] For example, two sheets in the Royal Collection, Windsor; Popham (1946), nos. 86 and 87.

Vittore Carpaccio

(b. Venice *c.* 1465; d. Venice 1525/26)

5 Head of a Woman in profile

Verso: Head of a Woman

Black chalk shaded with the point of the brush in brown wash and heightened with white, on pale blue-grey paper. 238 × 184.

Collections:

Richardson; Sir Anthony Westcombe, Bart; Bernard Granville; Sir John Charles Robinson; John Malcolm of Poltalloch; Hon. A. E. Gathorne-Hardy; by descent to the Hon. Robert Gathorne-Hardy. Accepted by H. M. Government *in lieu* of death duties, and allocated to the Ashmolean Museum in 1977.

Selected literature:

Lauts, no. Dr. 8; Muraro, p. 35; Macandrew, no. 8A.

We know more about Carpaccio's style and practice as a draughtsman than we do of his Venetian contemporaries, Giovanni Bellini or Alvise Vivarini: a variety of drawings, from compositional sketches to figure studies and workshop copies, have survived. This is one of the most beautiful of his drawings, and is a sheet of considerable importance. Blue paper was regularly used by Carpaccio in his head and figure studies, and this example has retained a good deal of its original freshness of colour. The artist used the same technique for the graceful profile on the *recto* and the pensive head on the *verso*: a fine black chalk was first employed, then the tonal range was increased by the use of thin strokes of brown wash for the hair and shadows on the flesh, and by touches of pure white as highlights.

Both studies were used by Carpaccio for his altar-piece of the *Presentation in the Temple*, signed and dated 1510, for the church of S. Giobbe, Venice, now in the Accademia: the heads of the two attendants of the Virgin closely correspond. However, the study on the *verso* was certainly used for one of the saints in the left foreground of the *Glory of St Ursula* altar-piece, also in the Accademia. Given the character of the head on the *recto*, and the separate study of the pennant, it is quite likely that this too was made in connexion with the same altar-piece. The painting accompanied Carpaccio's great narrative cycle for the Scuola di Sant'Orsola, adjacent to SS. Giovanni e Paolo. The scenes from the saint's life date from late 1490–95; despite the date of 1491 on the altar-piece there are good reasons for dating it closer to 1510, and the present altar-piece may have replaced the 1491 picture.[1] The drawing certainly could not be dated earlier than 1505, and is more likely to be later. Carpaccio's controlled graphic style, his careful modelling of form and study of the effects of light on these full faces, illustrate both his interest in naturalism, and his desire to exploit the full potential of his chosen technique. These interests matured as a result of Carpaccio's acquaintance with the work of Dürer: the German artist made two trips to Venice, in 1494–95 and in 1505–07.

---

[1] For a full discussion, see Pedrocco in Pignatti (1981), p. 88.

Michelangelo Buonarroti

(b. Caprese 1475; d. Rome, 1564)

6   Nude male Torso

Pen and brown ink with, and over, black chalk.
262 × 173.

Verso: Composition of two nude Men and a Horse

Black chalk.

Collections:
>   Sir Peter Lely; William Gibson; Jonathan Richardson, Senior (L. 2183); Benjamin West (L. 419); Sir Thomas Lawrence (L. 2445); Samuel Woodburn. Presented in 1846.

Selected literature:
>   Parker, II, no. 296; Dussler, no. 344; Hartt nos. 32 (*verso*), 35 (*recto*); Gere & Turner (1975), no. 10 (*verso*); Tolnay, no. 41.

This double-sided sheet of studies is probably connected with Michelangelo's preparations for the *Battle of Cascina*, commissioned around mid-1504 as a companion piece to the mural painting by Leonardo of the *Battle of Anghiari*, begun in 1503, on the wall of the Sala del Gran Consiglio in the Palazzo Vecchio. Republican Florence wished to celebrate earlier victories against the Milanese and the Pisans respectively. Michelangelo's work, interrupted in 1505 and 1506, was not carried out in fresco; his cartoon for the central group of *Bathers* is known through a copy.[1] This showed nude soldiers surprised by the Pisan attack while bathing, and the artist also had in mind scenes of cavalry and foot-soldiers in the middle distance.

The *verso* study shows a horse and two men, one mounting the horse and the other seen from behind as though holding the stirrup for his companion. It is quickly drawn in black chalk, and on the other side of the sheet, Michelangelo examined more closely the torso of one of the figures from a slightly different angle. Again, he used black chalk first, shading in some parts; then, with the pen, he followed the movements of the muscles in curving, rhythmic strokes, with very little cross-hatching, achieving an effect of Leonardesque fluidity. The drawing might be a life-study, although it is not clear where the right leg would stand, nor is the position an easy one to hold. Michelangelo's concentration on the torso may have been stimulated by his study of fragments of antique statuary. However, in many of his later life-studies, he tended to omit the head or other parts of the body which were not relevant to his immediate purpose.

---

[1] By Aristotile da Sangallo (oil on panel, 76.4 × 130.2 cm); collection of the Earl of Leicester, Holkham Hall, Norfolk.

Michelangelo

7   Page from a Sketch-book

Pen and brown ink. 137 × 142.

Collections:

William Young Ottley; Sir Thomas
Lawrence; Samuel Woodburn. Presented in 1846.

Selected literature:

Parker, II, no. 303; Dussler, no. 608; Hartt,
no. 120; Gere & Turner (1975), no. 28; Tolnay,
no. 170; Hirst (1989), no. 12.

Eight pages from a small sketchbook, long since dismembered, are in the Ashmolean's collection, in which Michelangelo explored a variety of ideas for the Sistine decoration.[1] As well as quick jottings with the pen, on a thumbnail scale as in this sheet, there are relatively large-scale figure studies in black chalk on some sheets, which are developments of the first ideas, and probably made from life. Not all of the figures were used in the frescoes, but those which can be identified all relate to the later part of the ceiling, and particularly to the *Ancestors of Christ* scenes in the lunettes. The conjunction of studies for the second stage of work, and some other evidence for dating the sheets to 1510–11, demonstrate that Michelangelo did not plan the details of the entire ceiling in advance, but rather began making designs for the second part after the unveiling of the first in 1510. After that experience, he was able to work rapidly on the remainder of the project. These pages convey the excitement and creative energy of the master as he put his mind to the task in hand.[2]

Prominent on the recto at the top left is an early idea for the figure of the prophet Jonah in the spandrel of the ceiling. On the right, in a darker shade of ink, is a vigorously drawn study of an old man, chin on hand, his beard jutting forward, who carries a broad-brimmed hat on his back. The lunette shape is clearly indicated. Michelangelo reversed the figure in its final form in the *Salmon-Booz-Obeth* lunette, accentuating the beard and adding a curiously headed walking stick. Amongst the figures on the *verso* is that of a sleeping youth, who was to be studied in reverse in a black chalk sketch on another page,[3] and who appeared in the destroyed *Phares-Esrom-Aram* lunette on the altar wall. The standing figure sketched faintly, lower left, and studied again on the right, is an idea for the figure of the woman looking in a mirror in the *Naason* lunette. Parker connected the reclining nude figure above with the *ignudo* to the left of the prophet Jeremiah; however, Hirst suggests that this was not used for the ceiling, and sees it as anticipating the design of the *Allegories* in the Medici Chapel.

Verso. Michelangelo, *Figure Studies*

[1] Parker, II, nos. 299–306.
[2] See Hirst (1986).
[3] Parker, II, no. 305.

Michelangelo

8 Head of a bearded Man shouting

Red chalk. 155 × 126.

Collections:

Duca di Modena; Sir Thomas Lawrence (L. 2445); Samuel Woodburn. Presented in 1846.

Selected literature:

Parker, II, no. 322; Dussler, no. 600; Hartt, no. 156; Gere & Turner (1975), no. 93; Tolnay, no. 310.

Anger is personified by this grotesque figure, who shouts, beard quivering, with his tense hand clutching his breast in emphasis. Michelangelo may have been thinking of a shouting head in profile in Leonardo's *Battle of Anghiari*;[1] however, this elderly character, with a soft hat askew on his head and eyes curiously squint, has a more comical air. Instead, the impact of Leonardo's studies of the passions is seen more fully in a highly worked drawing of the early 1520s, *Fury (Il Dannato)*, now in the Uffizi, one of three 'teste divine', divine heads which, Vasari tells us, Michelangelo made for his friend Gherardo Perini. *Fury* shows an open mouthed, crazed figure who has been described as a Dantesque lost soul.[2] By contrast, this shouting man is a more mundane figure; indeed, Tolnay has interpreted it as an ironical self-portrait, where the artist voices his frustration and anger.

The Ashmolean drawing was probably made around 1525. Michelangelo made use of the same idea in another sheet in the British Museum[3] (which has an ideal head of a woman, drawn in 1525–28, on the *recto*) in a humorous sketch probably made as part of a drawing lesson. This sketch clearly refers to Leonardo's profile head, but as a visual joke, for the young man's mouth gapes impossibly wide, and there are grotesque excrescences beneath his jaw. (The joke may be carried further with the squatting figure drawn immediately below.) The drawing lesson is one context in which the Ashmolean work can be viewed. Here, beneath the hat, at least one study of an eye and eyebrow can be discerned when the page is turned sideways. This is typical of the drawing exercises found on several sheets of the 1520s, in which the pupils copied the master's prototypes of eyes, heads or other motifs. Michelangelo often drew over his pupil's more feeble efforts. Thus, this study of anger, an emotion difficult to characterize, drawn with technical virtuosity, could have been set down as an exemplar by the master.

However, immediately to the left of the principal head is a fragment of another head study, this time of a younger man turned slightly to the left, whose hair, right eye, jawline, neck and collar can be seen. This detail, which has not been noticed before, suggests that the sheet was once larger, and the fact that the very important detail of the hand is only partially seen supports this possibility. (Interestingly, a study of a young man with a heart shaped face also appears on verso of the British Museum sheet.) Hence, the angry man could have been part of a group of two or perhaps three heads or half-length figures, where Michelangelo concentrated on this motif in particular, and lightly sketched one or two accompanying figures as a foil. This approach can be seen in another of the drawings for Perini, the *Venus, Mars and Cupid* in the Uffizi,[4] where the highly worked study of Venus is set between two sketchy contrasting heads. In a drawing of a very different sort, although of the same period, which is also in the Ashmolean,[5] Michelangelo sketched in pen and ink *Three Men in Conversation*, showing a heated exchange with appropriate rhetorical gestures, in what has been seen as a rare exercise in genre. Perhaps the same kind of interest informed the red chalk drawing, which was undoubtedly made with a witty intent.

---

[1] Cf. the drawing at Budapest; Popham (1946), no. 199.
[2] Tolnay, no. 306 recto.
[3] Tolnay, no. 316 verso; Wilde, no. 42.
[4] Tolnay, no. 307 recto.
[5] Parker, II, no. 326.

Michelangelo

9 The Worship of the Brazen Serpent

Red chalk. 244 × 335.

Collections:

Casa Buonarroti; J.-B.-J. Wicar; Sir Thomas Lawrence (L. 2445); Samuel Woodburn. Presented in 1846.

Selected literature:

Parker, II, no. 318; Dussler, no. 195; Hartt, no. 257; Gere & Turner (1975), no. 105; Tolnay, no. 266.

The two scenes drawn on this page have been identified as episodes from the Old Testament (Numbers 21. 4–9), showing the *Plague of Serpents* above and *The Cure of the Stricken* below. The drawing was probably made *c.* 1530, but we do not know of any related project in painting or sculpture.

Above, figures are struggling against, and fleeing from, the serpents in a dynamic composition whose movement spirals outwards from the centre. A magnificent muscular figure in the foreground curls up in agony as a serpent attacks his thigh; further to the right, a figure with one arm upraised, his body twisting in a typical *figura serpentinata*, heroically defends another. The red chalk is manipulated to marvellous effect, heightening the atmosphere of panic and terror. In the second scene, we see the edges of a crowd, which is treated with great economy; figures push and lean forward to witness the miracle of deliverance. This composition is more tightly knit, and treated almost as a low relief. Two men lift up a third, who turns to look above the heads of the crowd. This is reminiscent of an idea the artist explored much earlier when working on the *Battle of Cascina*.[1] This motif is highly worked, with the contours strengthened, adding to the polished, sculptural feel of this group.

The subjects are appropriate for a funerary chapel, or for church decoration, with the story of *Moses and the Brazen Serpent* viewed as a prefiguration of Salvation. Michelangelo had earlier included that subject in the Sistine Chapel decoration. It has been suggested that the artist had two scenes for lunettes in mind; one theory is that he may have intended to paint in fresco the lunettes above the tombs of the *Capitani* in the Medici Chapel at S. Lorenzo.[2] However, this seems unlikely as the spaces were probably intended for relief sculpture. Further, Joannides[3] argues that neither scene on this page was intended for a lunette format, but that Michelangelo had two rectangular compositions in mind, with which two drawings at Düsseldorf[4] may be associated. Another possiblity was proposed by Parker, who argued that because of the way in which the two scenes are placed on the page with some red chalk indications on the right, both could be studies for the left hand part of a larger composition.

---

[1] British Museum, London, and Musée du Louvre, Paris; Tolnay, nos. 46 *recto* and 47 *recto*.
[2] Tolnay, no. 266 discusses, with further elaboration, this theory proposed by A. E. Popp.
[3] In a letter of 18 February 1991.
[4] Dussler, nos. 393 and 394.

10   Samson and Delilah

Red chalk over indications in lead-point.
272 × 395.

Collections:

Casa Buonarroti; J.-B.-J. Wicar; Sir Thomas
Lawrence (L. 2445); Samuel Woodburn. Presented
in 1846.

Selected literature:

Parker, II, no. 319; Dussler, no. 624; Hartt,
no. 466; Gere & Turner (1975), no. 121; Tolnay,
no. 297.

Michelangelo almost certainly made this very beautiful drawing as an independent work, probably a presentation drawing. The artist gave as gifts to intimate friends some elaborate drawings, including superb head studies (which Vasari refers to as 'teste divine') from the early 1520s, and, from around 1530, some rather more ambitious allegorical and mythological compositions. These presentation drawings were tokens of love and friendship. They were slowly and carefully crafted, in black or red chalk, and they demanded equally slow and attentive perusal to appreciate their high quality and virtuoso draughtsmanship. Vasari lists four drawings of mythologial subjects which Michelangelo made in the 1530s for his close friend, the young Roman nobleman Tommaso de'Cavalieri: *The Punishment of Tityus*; *The Rape of Ganymede*; *The Fall of Phaeton* and a *Bacchanal of Children*. He also gave Tommaso 'teste divine' to help him learn to draw. Cavalieri probably inspired a good deal of Michelangelo's poetry, and many more of his elaborate drawings than Vasari records.

The narrative presentation drawings often have slightly mysterious or enigmatic themes, or are of subjects which can have an allegorical meaning. This Old Testament subject is open to interpretation as a story of love and betrayal, or of a hero who eventually fulfils his destiny, but the artist here chose to show the giant in a tormented moment, that of the recognition of the loss of his strength. Michelangelo took great care with the execution of the drawing, first indicating the contours of the great figure of Samson with lead-point, before working delicately and subtly with the orange-red chalk. This figure is highly finished, while that of Delilah is more lightly drawn as a dramatic foil to the main protagonist.

Raffaello Sanzio, called Raphael

(b. Urbino 1483; d. Rome 1520)

11   Portrait of the Artist

Grey-black chalk, heightened with white (somewhat oxidized) on discoloured white paper. 381 × 261.

Inscribed along the bottom margin in an ?eighteenth century hand:
> *Ritratto di se medissimo quando Giovane*

Collections:
   J.-B.-J. Wicar; William Young Ottley; Jeremiah Harman; Samuel Woodburn. Presented in 1846.

Selected literature:
   Fischel, no. 1; Parker, II, no. 515; Gere & Turner (1983), no. 34; Joannides, no. 9.

Traditionally, this has been identified as a self-portrait by Raphael, which would give the drawing a date of *c.* 1500 at the latest, since the sitter's age is no more than sixteen. The young man looks directly at the viewer, as is usual in self-portraits where the artist would have been looking in a mirror whilst drawing. The sitter also resembles the Raphael we know from the self-portrait some years later in the *School of Athens* fresco.

It has been argued by many Raphael scholars, however, that the style of the drawing suggests a later date of *c.* 1504, so that it cannot be a self-portrait.[1] Raphael's head studies at the time of the Brera *Sposalizio* display the same delicate handling of black chalk, and the same distilled purity of vision which is perceived as belonging to the end of his Umbrian period. On the other hand, the drawing, although accomplished, is in fact rather tentative. The contour of the face has been drawn and redrawn until a fuller sense of volume and proportion was achieved; the neck is still a little too long, despite corrections at the collar, while the shadowing of the nose and the side of the face, though sensitively drawn, does not show the sureness of touch and the ability to convey form which was certainly characteristic of Raphael by 1504. Portrait drawing, whether of oneself or a companion, is an obviously useful practice in the training period of any artist. On balance, the traditional view of the drawing seems to be the right one.

---

[1] For further references, see Gere & Turner (1983), under no. 34.

Raphael

12   Studies for two Guards in a Resurrection

Metal-point, heightened with white, on greyish-green prepared paper. 320 × 220.

Collections:
    Duque de Alva; Sir Thomas Lawrence
(L. 2445); Samuel Woodburn. Presented in 1846.

Selected literature:
    Fischel (1917), no. 74; Parker, II, no. 505;
Gere & Turner (1983), no. 14; Joannides, no. 27.

These two figures were drawn from the life, with studio assistants in every-day dress posing as models. The standing figure corresponds with the figure of a soldier in a painting of the *Resurrection* of *c.* 1502 from the studio of Perugino, now in the São Paolo Museum, Brazil. The seated figure could be an early idea for a soldier in the left foreground of the picture, who is also seated on a circular shield. Another drawing in the same technique by Raphael, which is also in the Ashmolean,[1] includes a study of a reclining figure which corresponds with that of a guard in the same picture. Raphael had a close association with Perugino and his workshop which continued even while he produced paintings as an independent master from around 1499. Here it seems that he worked on some of the initial designs for the picture, which another artist would execute, just as in the same period he produced compositional drawings for Pintoricchio's decoration of the Piccolomini Library at Siena.

Fundamental to Raphael's training was the mastery of drawing in metal-point, and he made this traditional tool his own, continuing to use it in his maturity long after other artists had discarded it as inflexible. In this relatively early drawing, Raphael achieves a vigorous, elastic contour which endows the striding figure with solidity and grace. Perugino's influence is still visible in the younger artist's simplified, geometric approach; nevertheless, a sharpness of observation, and a keenness to capture tension and weight in these figures distinguish Raphael's life studies from those of his senior (see no. 2).

[1] Parker, II, no. 506.

46

Raphael

13 A Group of Musicians

Pen and brown ink. 232 × 185.

Verso: The dead Christ carried to the Tomb

Pen and brown ink, pricked for transfer.

Collections:
     J.-B.-J. Wicar; William Young Ottley; Sir Thomas Lawrence; Samuel Woodburn.

Selected literature:
     Fischel, no. 89; Parker, II, no. 525; Gere & Turner (1983), no. 47; Joannides, no. 135.

The musical instruments are only summarily indicated in this unusual group: the elegant figure on the right, possibly identifiable as Apollo, plays what could be a rebec; the female figure – a Muse? – plays a harp, while a curly-headed youth, who, if classical references are intended, could be Bacchus, sounds a type of slide-trombone. Raphael may have intended to make separate studies of the instruments; his concern here was with the rhythmic relationship of the figures. The drawing dates from *c.* 1505, when Raphael was in Florence; it may well be associated with another Ashmolean drawing, *A Group of Vintagers*, also in pen and ink, which again shows three figures, two female and one male, and displays the same kind of handling and interest in flattened forms.[1] That drawing is squared for enlargement. Joannides suggested that both might be connected with the decoration of a musical instrument. Fischel associated the two designs with another similar drawing on the same scale, *A Group of Four Standing Warriors*,[2] and argued that all three were studies for the decoration of a palace façade. Neither of these theories can be verified. Raphael's working methods are characterized by their efficiency and economy; he rarely wasted his efforts, and his drawings on the whole tend to have been made with a particular purpose in mind.

On the *verso* of this sheet is a preparatory study for Raphael's *Entombment* altar-piece of 1507, now in the Borghese Gallery, Rome. This is one of a sequence of drawings in which the artist studied the action of carrying Christ's body to the tomb: here he examined the relation of the upper part of the body and arm to the left hand bearer. The study is pricked for the transfer of this motif to another sheet of paper for further development – an instance of Raphael's economical working methods – and this confirms that the recto drawing was made earlier, as Raphael would not have used a sheet disfigured by pricking for that careful study.

Verso. Raphael, *The dead Christ carried to the Tomb*

[1] Parker, II, no. 524.
[2] Parker, II, no. 523.

Raphael

14 A Combat of nude Men

Red chalk over preliminary stylus work.
379 × 281.

Collections:
J.-B.-J. Wicar; William Young Ottley; Sir
Thomas Lawrence (L. 2445); Samuel Woodburn.
Presented in 1846.

Selected literature:
Fischel, no. 309; Parker, II, no. 552; Gere
& Turner (1983), no. 102; Joannides, no. 233.

Raphael made extensive preparatory studies for the decoration of the Stanza della Segnatura in the Vatican, which was his first Papal commission, the success of which determined the course of his career. The knowledge that Michelangelo was at work nearby in the Sistine Chapel must have acted as a further stimulus to the display of his abilities. This magnificent study was drawn in preparation for a detail of the *School of Athens*, painted *c.* 1509: the combat appears in a feigned marble bas-relief beneath the statue of Apollo at the left of the fresco.

Perhaps Raphael knew of his rival's red chalk life studies for his fresco. Although he had taken up the medium in Florence, Raphael had on the whole studied the male nude with the pen: indeed, the close, precise working of the sharp stick of chalk here is reminiscent of his penwork. The figures were first drawn with the stylus, whose indentations can clearly be seen in the upper parts of the forms, which are more highly worked. The roughly sketched shouting figure was added as a foil to the figure on the right, perhaps as an afterthought as no underdrawing is visible. Raphael's increased command of the male nude is apparent in this powerful drawing, although his emphasis on graceful movement and formal patterning is still stronger than his interest in individual anatomy and muscularity.

The Stanza della Segnatura was apparently intended to house Julius II's personal library; it was essentially a private room for the Pope and his intimates. It was in this period that Raphael began to collaborate with Marcantonio Raimondi as a means of bringing his talents to a wider audience. This study of the heroic male nude in action may have stimulated Raphael towards planning his virtuoso composition, the *Massacre of the Innocents* of *c.* 1511, intended for publication as a print.[1]

---

[1] Bartsch, XIV, pp. 19–20, no. 18.

Raphael

15 Two nude Studies

Black chalk, heightened with white (oxidized), on brownish (discoloured) paper. 257 × 362.

Collections:
> Duque de Alva; Sir Thomas Lawrence; Samuel Woodburn. Presented in 1846.

Selected literature:
> Parker, II, no. 569; Fischel & Oberhuber no. 487; Gere & Turner (1983), no. 181; Joannides, no. 441; Gere, no. 40.

These life studies were part of Raphael's preparatory work for the painting of the *Battle of the Milvian Bridge* in the Sala di Costantino in the Vatican. His senior assistants, Giulio Romano and Gianfrancesco Penni, won the commission from Pope Leo X after Raphael's death, as they held the master's designs, and could be entrusted to execute his grand and noble concepts. In fact, there were long delays, and changes in plan, while the workshop gradually diverged from many of Raphael's original designs.

The figures are preparatory for those of two soldiers straining to prevent themselves from drowning by pulling themselves into a boat; in the fresco, their positions are transposed. Raphael characteristically made a light sketch first with the stylus for the left hand figure, but drew the second figure directly in black chalk. His use of the medium is versatile and economical: he explored the fall of light on tensed muscles here, but also suggested, through his rubbing of the chalk and his use of the white, the sense of wet bodies and reflected water. Raphael displayed a renewed interest in Leonardo da Vinci at this stage of his career (he intended to use an oil-based medium for the apartment, and must have recalled Leonardo's *Battle of Anghiari* in his thoughts on the decoration), and in this drawing sought *sfumato* and painterly effects. Both the expressive and the narrative roles these figures would have in the final picture are already visible in this superb drawing.

Raphael's workshop was run on efficient lines: this kind of life study was preliminary to a full compositional design, which Penni would draft, while Giulio based his full scale figure studies on models such as these. Although few drawings survive for the commission, it is clear from this study that Raphael's plans had reached an advanced stage.

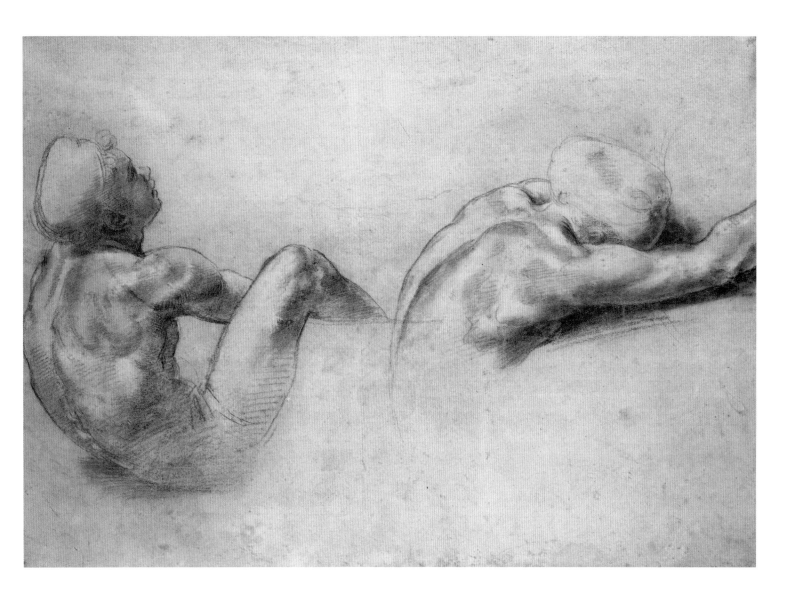

Tiziano Vecellio, called Titian

(b. Pieve di Cadore *c.* 1484/88; d. Venice 1576)

16 A Horse and Rider falling

Black chalk on grey paper, squared in red chalk.
274 × 262.

Inscribed:
> *T.an; Titiano; T.*

Collections:
> Nicholas Lanier (L. 2886); Jonathan Richardson Senior (L. 2184); Benjamin West (L. 419); Sir Thomas Lawrence (L. 2445); William Esdaile (L. 2617); Revd Dr Henry Wellesley; Josiah Gilbert. Presented by Mrs Josiah Gilbert in 1895.

Selected literature:
> Parker, II, no. 718; Parker (1958), no. 20; Sutton, no. 15; Wethey (1987), no. 5c; Chiari, no. 25; Venice, *Tiziano*, no. 29b.

Titian captures a moment of energetic movement here: the twisting horse falls to the ground, while its rider strains backwards in order to ward off an attack. The black chalk is used with great verve and freedom, with some white highlighting added to sharpen the effect of flexing movement and tension; some details have been deepened and strengthened with the black so as to indicate the overall tonal values of the final work. The squaring-up of the drawing suggests that Titian was ready to move on to the next stage of work on a larger scale, possibly on the canvas itself.

The drawing is a preparatory study for a detail in the left foreground of Titian's large *Battle* for the Sala del Maggior Consiglio in the Palazzo Ducale at Venice, commissioned in 1513 but not carried out until mid 1537–mid 1538. The picture was destroyed in the fire of 1577, but its composition is known through copies. There has been much discussion about the subject of the picture: it has been argued that it showed the *Battle of Cadore*, a Venetian victory of 1508, or (the more likely alternative) the *Battle of Spoleto* of 1155.[1]

The relationship of this drawing to the lost painting has also been debated, in that it does not correspond precisely to the relevant detail in the final composition. However, Titian's designs did not by any means reach a decisive stage on paper: unlike his Roman or Florentine contemporaries, he often clarified his ideas on the canvas itself, even making radical changes while a painting was well under way. We know of a vigorous compositional drawing for the *Battle*, now in the Musée du Louvre,[2] where the left foreground includes a horseman charging on a rearing horse. Titian transformed this idea into a skirmish of two horsemen, and he explored the main elements in the Ashmolean sheet. By the time of the painting, he had altered his concept to show instead the rider as a more strongly silhouetted figure, with the horse's head now bowed.

---

[1] See Wethey (1975), pp. 225–29 on this subject, and a summary of his arguments in Wethey (1987), pp. 67–68. Amongst other copies are two in the Ashmolean, also given by Mrs Gilbert: a drawing attributed to Martino Rota, Parker, II, no. 674; and an anonymous painting, A277.
[2] Wethey (1987), no. 5. There is a comparable drawing, of a rearing horseman, a study for another detail in the same painting, at Munich; Wethey (1987), no. 5b.

Andrea d'Agnolo, called Andrea del Sarto

(b. Florence 1486/88; d. Florence 1530/31)

17 Study of an old Woman's Head

Red chalk. 250 × 186.

Collections:
J.-B.-J. Wicar; Sir Thomas Lawrence (L. 2445); Samuel Woodburn. Presented in 1846.

Selected literature:
Parker, II, no. 692; Freedberg, under no. 83; Shearman, II, p. 367; Sutton, no. 22.

There is no doubt that Andrea del Sarto drew this worn, pensive female head from the life. The strength of red chalk as a medium for conveying the qualities of human flesh is well illustrated here: the sunken eyes and cheeks, the wrinkled forehead and skinny neck are all vividly expressed. The drawing is a preparatory study for the figure of St Elizabeth in the *Madonna and Child with St Elizabeth and the Infant St John* of c. 1529, made for Ottaviano de'Medici and now in the Palazzo Pitti. In the painting, the saint is a somewhat younger and more idealized figure, and wears a veil rather than the sketchily indicated cap here. The picture was a celebrated one, and several versions and copies are known.

The artist's sharp eyes and keen observation can be seen in numerous surviving life drawings, many of which are informal, rapid studies in red chalk or pen and ink. Sarto was deeply concerned with naturalism, more so than many of his contemporaries, and is the heir to Leonardo in his studies of expression and physiognomy. The intense concentration he brought to bear on this life study, where the grim, sour mood was not appropriate for the projected sacred figure, speaks eloquently of his interests.

Sarto was greatly admired as a draughtsman: he ran an important studio, with Jacopo Pontormo, Rosso Fiorentino and Francesco Salviati among his pupils, but his drawings were also highly influential for a wider circle of artists, including Giovanni Battista Naldini (see no. 22). There is a copy of the Ashmolean drawing, attributed to Salviati, in the Fitzwilliam Museum, Cambridge (inv. no. 3134).

Girolamo Francesco Maria Mazzola, called Parmigianino

(b. Parma 1503; d. Casal Maggiore 1540)

18 A young Pilgrim seated on the Ground

Red chalk. 165 × 152.

Collections:

?Cavaliere Francesco Baiardo; Benjamin West (L. 419); Sir Thomas Lawrence (L. 2445); George Richmond. Purchased in 1953.

Selected literature:

Parker, II, no. 437; Popham (1971), no. 332.

A young man is seated on the ground, removing his shoes. The greater part of his body is in shadow, but a pilgrim's shell can be seen on his right shoulder (a shell provided a convenient drinking vessel during long journeys) and a staff lies in the shadowed area beside him. Popham remarked that the figure could represent that of Moses removing his shoes before the burning bush; however, the attributes of a pilgrim are clear, and they are attributes shared by a traveller, St Roch, who is invoked principally against the plague.

Parmigianino was a great innovator, and did not by any means confine himself to standard representations of subjects. He was also a brilliant and prolific draughtsman, who made quick, inventive sketches for their own sake, as well as in preparation for paintings. This is certainly an early drawing, dating from before his visit to Rome in 1524. Because of the sensuous handling of the red chalk, and the apprehension of the figure in terms of light and shadow, the drawing was attributed to Correggio until Parker identified it as by Parmigianino. As Popham noted, it may be the drawing, no. 309, described in the inventory of Parmigianino's patron, the Cavaliere Francesco Baiardo, as a red chalk drawing of St Roch taking off his shoes ('Un disegno di San Rocca che si calza le scarpe...').

This idea of a bent, shadowed figure concentrating on a mundane action which is picked out by the fall of light was taken up again by the artist in a slightly later red chalk drawing of a man removing his breeches.[1]

[1] Musée Turpin de Crissé, Angers; Huchard & Laing, no. 79, pl. 73.

Francesco de Rossi, called Salviati

(b. Florence 1510; d. Rome, 1563)

19 Design for a Ewer

Pen and brown ink with grey wash, heightened with body-colour, over black chalk on buff paper. 411 × 276.

Collections:
Gelozzi (L. 545); Viscount Hampden. Francis Douce, by whom bequeathed in 1834.

Selected literature:
Parker, II, no. 683; Hayward, pp. 144, 345.

Salviati was a highly inventive and sophisticated artist whose services as decorator and designer were much in demand. He worked for the Medici and the Farnese, and besides travelling between Florence, Rome and Venice, he was sought after by the French court, where he finally spent some time in the mid-1550s. He was a virtuoso draughtsman, as this brilliantly executed sheet demonstrates.

The artist was closely associated with goldsmiths, having trained in the craft. A large number of his designs for intricately worked luxury objects – of which this is one of the finest – are known, although the ewers, basins, fan-handles and other objects have not, as a rule, survived. This drawing displays an essentially Late Mannerist taste for magnificent designs which combine the beautiful and the bizarre, and antique motifs with modern fantasy. Such elements appear on a variety of Mannerist decorative work, from the applied arts to tapestry and fresco. The conceit of making use of the three Graces, one of them acting as a handle, is particularly apt. Furthermore, the drawing is a superbly finished work in itself, as an evocation of a marvellously wrought object, with the light playing on its gleaming surface, and as such rises far above any practical function it may have had.

Lelio Orsi

(b. Reggio 1511; d. Novellara 1587)

20   The Conversion of St Paul

Pen and brown ink, squared for enlargement in plumbago. 457 × 301 (arched at top).

Collections:
  ?the Gonzagas at Novellara; Earl of Gainsborough. Purchased in 1955.

Selected literature:
  Parker, II, no. 420*; Macandrew, no. 422A; Monducci & Pirondini, no. 125.

This is a highly finished compositional drawing, in which even the smallest detail of the figures, horses and clouds has been worked up with precision and finesse. The landscape background, which includes some classical remains, is also very fully indicated. The impact of Michelangelo's fresco of the same subject in the Cappella Paolina on the design and individual figures is obvious; indeed, it is as though Orsi set himself the challenge of inventing a thoroughly Michelangelesque composition, executed with a virtuoso technique.[1] The central motif of the terrified horses, struggling out of control of the soldiers, is particularly striking. However, it is typical of Orsi's idiosyncratic, even Mannerist, approach to composition that the dynamism and the technical prowess displayed in this group draws our attention away from the principal theme.

Lelio worked mainly in Novellara and Reggio Emilia, as a painter, architect and designer of metalwork. However, he visited Rome in 1554–55, and his strong interest in Michelangelo becomes apparent from then on. The fact that he asked in a letter of 1559 for a drawing of the Cappella Paolina to be sent from Rome has been linked to this composition (although we do not know what sort of drawing he wanted). No connected painting is known, but Orsi treated the subject in other drawings.[2] He produced some miniature paintings on parchment, and the meticulous treatment of this design may have led to the suggestion that the artist had such a small picture in mind. However, the drawing is squared up, which is generally preparatory to transfer to a larger scale; if it can be associated with the letter of 1559, then Orsi must have been working on an important commission. Vittoria Romani has argued for a connexion with a possible commission for the Carmelite church at Novellara; as yet, this has proved inconclusive.[3]

[1] See Olszewski, no. 87, for a copy of no. 20 mentioned by Macandrew, and for further suggestions as to Orsi's sources for the composition, which he dates c. 1580.
[2] Two drawings are in the British Museum; Popham (1967), nos. 50 and 51. A miniature copy, with variations, is in the Galleria Estense, Modena.
[3] Romani, pp. 41–44.

Jacopo Robusti, called Tintoretto

(b. Venice 1518; d. Venice 1594)

21   Samson slaying the Philistines, after Michelangelo

Black chalk, touched with white, on faded blue paper. 418 × 275.

Collections:
> William Bates (L. 2604). Purchased in 1939.

Selected literature:
> Parker, II, no. 714; Rossi, p. 14, as School of Tintoretto.

Tintoretto's energetic study is one of a group of drawings after Michelangelo, now in various collections. Jacopo did not travel south to see any of his great mentor's sculpture, but he knew and studied a good deal of it through copies and casts. Daniele da Volterra, a friend and follower of Michelangelo, certainly sent Tintoretto casts and small *modelli*, including the four allegories of the Medici Chapel in S. Lorenzo.[1] Jacopo obtained, probably through the same source, a small wax or clay model of a group of wrestling figures, after Michelangelo's *Samson and the Philistines* (a project on which the master worked around 1530, but which was never executed). This model enabled him to study both Michelangelo's invention, and his muscular figure types; several drawings were made from it by Tintoretto and his pupils.[2] On the *verso* of this sheet is another study of the same group seen from the same angle.

Tintoretto made a habit of studying figures in the round: in preparation for his large narrative paintings, he would make models of the forms out of wax and clay, and would move them around in specially constructed boxes so as to examine the effects of light and shadow, and to arrive at the best compositional design. He drew the *Samson* group from a number of different angles: in another drawing in the Ashmolean,[3] the viewpoint is lower, and a wooden strut which supported the model is clearly visible.

This drawing is an extremely free and rapid study, where the group is depicted in terms of light and shade, in a very painterly manner. Thus, a line of demarcation has been subsequently added to separate Samson's back from the head of the Philistine, but the principal figure's left arm emerges subtly and gradually from this shadowed area. Yet Tintoretto was also keen to convey the fact that this is a piece of sculpture, made of a hard material which catches the light, and he did so in his use of white heightening. The quality of the drawing, and its bold handling, make it comparable with similar studies at Christ Church, Oxford.[4] Rossi's contention that no. 21 is a studio work is unconvincing.

[1] Ridolfi, II, p. 14.
[2] Rossi, pp. 13–15, and pl. 23–25.
[3] Parker, II, no. 713, a weaker drawing which may be by a pupil.
[4] Byam Shaw (1976), no. 763.

Giovanni Battista Naldini

(b. Florence 1537; d. Florence 1591)

22   Head of St Helena

Red chalk. 355 × 260.

Inscribed in ink:
   König, Vienne 1861; 9311; from Collection Praun à Nuremberg.

Verso: Three Saints

Inscribed in ink:
   Titian; Pa.

Pen and brown ink with brown and some grey wash.

Collections:
   Paul de Praun; Michelangelo Pacetti (L. 2057); Moriz König; Paul Davidsohn (L. 654); C. R. Rudolf (L. 2811[b]). Purchased in 1977 (Blakiston Fund).

Selected literature:
   Macandrew, no. 417A.

St Helena, the mother of the Emperor Constantine and a zealous Christian, is revered for her discovery of the Cross upon which Christ was crucified when she visited the Holy Land in 326. Naldini drew the saint here as an old woman, with a coronet signifying her rank, in this study for the figure of St Helena in a lost altar-piece. Elena Ottonelli (d. 1576) paid for the painting of *Christ in Glory with Saints Agnes, Helena and attendant saints* which was in the chapel of the Compagnia di S. Agnese in S. Maria del Carmine, Florence, but has been lost since the disastrous fire of 1771. Naldini's modello for the altar-piece is, however, in the Ashmolean.[1] The commission was apparently first given to Maso da San Friano (1531–1571), but passed to Naldini on his death. Drawings for the altar-piece by both artists are known, with Naldini making use of some of his predecessor's designs, while also looking to Vasari for some of the figures.

This is a particularly fine example of the artist's bold and confident drawing style, and may have been made from the life. The head of St Helena in the *modello* is at a slightly different angle; although treated very loosely there, the saint's features are more idealized. Naldini was a pupil of Pontormo's, and like him was stimulated by the drawings of Andrea del Sarto (see no. 17); he also had a long association with Vasari, working with him at the Palazzo Vecchio in Florence.

The predominant influence on the drawing on the *verso* is in fact that of Vasari. St Luke is seated between St Blaise and St Dominic in an outdoor setting, while a cherub bearing an inscription flies above. This is possibly a study for an altar-piece, although no related painting is known. A pen and ink drawing at Edinburgh[2] of the lower part of the composition with the group of three saints is clearly connected with this one, although the variations (particularly in the figure of St Blaise) suggest that it was derived from a different source, perhaps a more finished design or even a lost painting. That drawing has been convincingly attributed to Cristofano Gherardi (1508–1556), who collaborated extensively with Vasari in his later career.[3] The prototype may therefore have been a design by Vasari, which was circulating amongst his followers. If the *verso* drawing is by Naldini, it probably dates from 1565–71, when he was very close to Vasari. Thus, he simply re-used the sheet for the later study of St Helena, even though the grey wash shows through to the recto in a somewhat disfiguring manner. One problem with this theory is that the style and handling of the drawing seem uncharacteristic of Naldini; however, he was undoubtedly a versatile draughtsman and his authorship should not be excluded. The alternative, less likely explanation would be that the *verso* drawing is by another follower of Vasari who had access to the work of Naldini.

---

[1] A1014. For a discussion of the commission and a list of related drawings, see Lloyd (1977), pp. 129–32.
[2] Andrews, no. D3091.
[3] Monbeig Goguel, p. 114, note 14.

Jacopo Ligozzi

(b. Verona *c.* 1547; d. Verona 1632)

23   Allegory of the Earth

Pen and ink with wash, heightened with gold, on a brown preparation. 279 × 188.

Collections:
Benjamin West (L. 419); Charles Gasc (L. 544); J. P. Heseltine (L. 1508); Earl of Warwick (L. 2600); E. L. Paget. Purchased in 1946.

Selected literature:
Parker, II, no. 283.

Gaia, or Ge, the personification of the earth, is the subject of this highly polished drawing. She was venerated by the Greeks as a fertile, all-nourishing mother, while the Romans worshipped her under the name of Tellus. According to legend, she concealed her numerous children, who were hated by their father, Uranus, in the bosom of the earth. Hence the goddess here presses her breast, which signifies nourishment and protection, while her children emerge from the earth. A young girl in contemporary dress, who holds a flower (perhaps a reference to her name, or to a family emblem), looks on in wonder. The delicate technique, and the chosen colours, seem perfectly appropriate to the subject.

Ligozzi was a court painter to the Medici from 1577 to the end of his life, and was responsible for a wide range of activities, including decorative commissions and making designs for jewellery, glass, tapestries and furniture. His precision and sensitivity as a draughtsman aided the scientific studies of Francis I, for whom Ligozzi provided accurate drawings of animals and plants. The artist enjoyed working as a miniaturist and illustrator (he proudly signed himself 'miniator'), and often used gold to highlight his drawings, giving them a precious and luxurious quality. Indeed, many of his drawings were produced as independent works. Ligozzi was much influenced by Northern art, particularly by the chiaroscuro drawings and woodcuts of Altdorfer, Hans Baldung Grien, Burgkmair and others. However, as Parker pointed out, the technique of making highly finished monochrome studies heightened with gold was also one used by Mantegna.

Jacopo Palma il Giovane

(b. Venice 1548; d. Venice 1628)

24   A Merchant's Wife

Pen and brown ink and wash. 237 × 150 (irregular).

Collections:
   Bradbury; Revd Dr Henry Wellesley; Richard Johnson. Purchased in 1956.

Selected literature:
   Parker (1958), no. 66; Macandrew, no. 433A.

Unlike the majority of his Venetian contemporaries, Palma Giovane was an extremely prolific draughtsman. An early biographer, Carlo Ridolfi, wrote that Palma made an infinite number of drawings, many for their own sake as creative sketches; no sooner was the tablecloth removed after a meal than the artist was jotting his ideas down once again.[1] Certainly a very large number have come down to us, as Palma's work was popular among eighteenth century collectors. His formative years were spent in Rome, which accounts for the central importance of *disegno* in his career; characteristically, Palma collaborated on the production of two treatises on drawing, Odoardo Fialetti's *Il vero modo et ordine per dissegnar tutte le parti et membra del corpo umano* of 1608, and Giacomo Franco's *De excellentia et nobilitate delineationis libri duo* of 1611. Franco, an engraver, print dealer and publisher, was an intimate family friend.

Palma provided this image of a luxuriously dressed Venetian lady for another of Franco's projects, the *Habiti D'Huomeni et Donne Venetiane* of 1610, where it appears as no. 10, *Moglie di Mercante col Ventolino*. The engraver followed the drawing exactly, adding a curtain looped up behind; the image appears in reverse with respect to the drawing. A drawing at Christ Church, Oxford, which shows a fashionably dressed lady seated in a chair before a curtain, was probably for the same project, although it was not reproduced, and other drawings are known, in the Vienna Academy, Leningrad and elsewhere.[2] Palma's preferred drawing medium was pen, ink and wash. Here he cleverly evokes the different textures of the costume: the stiffness of the bodice, the weight of the fabric of skirt and sleeves, the transparency of the lace. The lady looks quizzically at the viewer, with a hint of flirtation. This doe-eyed, small-chinned female type recurs in other drawings by Palma, including one of a younger model dated 1596, now in the Pierpont Morgan Library, which has been identified as a portrait of the artist's daughter, Virginia.[3]

---

[1] Ridolfi, II, p. 203.
[2] see Byam Shaw (1976), under no. 823.
[3] see Schwarz, under no. 17.

Lodovico Carracci

(b. Bologna 1555; d. Bologna 1619)

25   Sleeping male Nude

Red chalk. 237 × 223.

Collections:

Richard Houlditch (L. 2214); Sir Thomas Lawrence (L. 2445); Samuel Woodburn; Lord Francis Egerton, by whom presented in 1853.

Selected literature:

Parker, II, no. 171; Mahon, no. 23; Bohn, p. 414; Degrazia, no. 117.

The air of spontaneity and mood of sunlit contentment in this life study are quite convincing; it is as though the model had fallen into a pleasant doze while lying, completely relaxed, on a comfortable surface, with the light pouring in from the left. Yet Lodovico set himself a challenge in capturing this difficult foreshortened pose. The red chalk is used with differing pressure to create shifting blocks of shadow, in a play of dark and light tones; a contour line, emphatic in the areas of greatest shadow, but almost disappearing in the lightest parts, gives sharper definition to the form. The weight of the body, and the impression it makes on the surface (some folds of a blanket or the like are indicated) are cleverly suggested. At some stage, possibly soon after it was made, the drawing was cut out of the original sheet and laid down on a new page, with the red chalk shading continued and expanded, perhaps by a pupil.

The Carracci are celebrated for the emphasis they placed on the practice of drawing, above all drawing from the life in order to train the hand, sharpen the observation and build up a vocabulary of forms. The life drawings of Lodovico and Annibale are sometimes hard to distinguish in the early 1580s, because of their shared aims and interests – both admired Correggio, for instance. However, the authorship of this study has not been disputed. Lodovico was particularly concerned in the mid-1580s with examining the effects of light on form, and in making strong contrasts of light and shade; some of his figures have a slightly rubbery appearance as a result. Dramatically foreshortened figures can be seen in some of his paintings of the later 1580s, such as those in *The Transfiguration*, in a private collection.[1]

---

[1] Washington, *The Age of Correggio and the Carracci*, no. 105.

Lodovico Carracci

26 The Birth of St John the Baptist

Black chalk with pen and brown ink and grey wash, heightened with a little white, on pale buff paper; indented for transfer and squared in black chalk. 356 × 567.

Collections:

Sir Thomas Lawrence (L. 2445); Lord Francis Egerton, Earl of Ellesmere (L. 2710[b]); by descent to the sixth Duke of Sutherland. Purchased in 1972, with the help of contributions from the Friends of the Ashmolean, the National Art-Collections Fund, the Pilgrim Trust, and the William A. Cadbury Charitable Trust.

Selected literature:

Mahon, no. 11; Macandrew, no. 194A; Bohn, under no. 6.

Lodovico drew this very elegant, balanced composition of nine figures in preparation for a painting of *The Birth of St John the Baptist*, probably of the early 1590s. The picture was last recorded as belonging to John Fitzpatrick (1745–1818), second Earl of Upper Ossory: Gavin Hamilton acquired it for him in Italy in early 1770. The composition of the painting is known from an engraving by Domenico Cunego of 1769, published in Hamilton's *Schola Italica Picturae* (Rome, 1773).

At this stage of the preparation, Lodovico was concerned with establishing the rhythm of the figure groups, and their actions and expressions. He used black chalk first (and various alterations can be seen, especially in the figure of the woman holding up the basin), then fixed the main lines of his design with pen, ink and wash. In the painting, the figures were placed in an echoing interior setting (which led Hamilton to detect, in a letter to his patron, the influence of Tintoretto), but the essentials of the figure group here remained. An interesting omission, however, is that of the maidservant, whose figure links the two main groups. Lodovico had actually studied this figure in detail, as a drawing in the Uffizi shows,[1] so that the change in composition was made at a very late stage. The Virgin Mary, Elizabeth's cousin, holds the child, watched by an older woman, while a maid reaches up to take him so as to wash him, and his father, Zacharias, kneels on the right; two maids bring water while a sibylline seated figure looks out at the viewer. Lodovico's continuing interest in the art of Correggio is manifest in many of the figure types and in their movements and gestures.

Evidently, the artist had some difficulty with the group of the Virgin and the old woman, as this whole section has been carefully cut out and re-patched, presumably with a revised design. (This cutting and patching must have happened at the time, because there are two pen and ink studies of legs on the *verso* which were clearly made after the patching, and these have been attributed by Mahon to Agostino. The only other explanation, that at some point in the drawing's later history the section was carefully cut out by a collector, and just as carefully replaced by the same or a subsequent owner, seems highly unlikely.) There are still some re-workings visible, to the old woman's figure in particular. Lodovico resolved this awkwardness in the painting, where the woman no longer tries to take hold of the child, but gazes at him, hands outspread in wonder.

---

[1] Bohn, no. 6.

Annibale Carracci

(b. Bologna 1560; d. Rome 1609)

27   A Semi-nude Boy

Red chalk, heightened with white, on buff paper.
277 × 192.

Collections:
    Galleria Simonetti (L. 2288[bis]). Purchased
in 1940.

Selected literature:
    Parker, II, no. 143; Ostrow; Posner, under
nos. 15, 21.

A smiling, half-draped boy holds an ambiguous pose in this life drawing, in which a number of possible actions can be read. The figure seems to be in motion, stepping up or down, while the way in which the muscles of the chest are tensed, together with the positions of the hands, suggest that an object is being carried, possibly concealed in the folds of the drapery. In fact, Annibale – a skilful and resourceful draughtsman – made use of this beautifully executed study in his preparation for two different commissions of the 1580s.

The boy appears, fully clad, in the left foreground of the fresco *The Infant Jason carried in a Coffin to Chiron's Cave* in the Palazzo Fava, Bologna, part of an important narrative cycle carried out as a collaborative effort by the three Carracci. Annibale painted this scene in 1584.[1] The pose and expression of the boy are very similar in the fresco, the principal change being in the angle of his arms, for he now holds a tall jug to his chest. The boy's appealing glance over his shoulder, and the curving fall of drapery from hip to knee as he walks, are directly transposed from the drawing. Annibale allowed for the fact that the light falls from the left in the fresco, adding some delicate touches of white on the drapery.

At the same time, Annibale was preparing for a major altar-piece, commissioned in October 1583,[2] the *Baptism of Christ* in S. Gregorio, Bologna, completed in 1585.[3] The Ashmolean drawing must have been made when Annibale was working on some ideas for the left foreground of that painting, where a young man is shown undressing. The adolescent model for that figure appears in another life drawing of a youth kneeling, who pulls up his shirt with both hands.[4] Annibale evidently decided upon a more complex pose for that figure, so as to complement the kneeling figure of Christ in the altar-piece. No. 27 clearly had a role to play in this procedure, because, although the young man is shown from another angle in the painting, his stance is essentially the same if one turns the model in the drawing clockwise through an angle of ninety degrees. The visualization of a carefully studied figure from another angle came easily to an artist so well versed in life drawing.

The artist's interest in Correggio at this time is clear in the drawing: as Ostrow pointed out, he placed the model in a pose reminiscent of Correggiesque motifs, while the softness of the modelling and the boy's charming expression also testify to Annibale's study of the older master.

[1] Posner, no. 15.
[2] Boschloo, II, p. 179, note 6.
[3] Posner, no. 21.
[4] Musée du Louvre, Paris; Bacou (1961), no. 25.

Guido Reni

(b. Bologna 1575; d. Bologna 1642)

28 The Mystic Marriage of St Catherine

Pen and brown ink and wash. 237 × 183.

Collections:
  purchased in 1955.

Selected literature:
  Parker, II, no. 934*; Macandrew, no. 934A.

Reni treats a popular but nonetheless mystical subject in a fresh and engaging manner in this early drawing. The symbolic marriage of the saint to the Christ Child denotes her privileged position in the sacred sphere, as well as recalling her earthly life of renunciation. The subject is usually treated as a reverent, intimate scene, or as part of a *sacra conversazione* with other saints present. Reni indicates a context that is at once informal, even cosily domestic, with St Joseph as a preoccupied father, and also spacious and majestic, with a grand sweep of drapery above and an elegant balustrade opening onto a townscape. If Reni had a painting in mind, it must have been a private devotional commission. The drawing probably dates from 1598–99, and a connexion has been suggested with a lost *Mystical Marriage of St Catherine* mentioned by Malvasia as being in the possession of the Bonfiglioli family.[1]

The drawing displays the impact of the lessons Reni had learned at the Carracci Academy, first from Agostino and then from Lodovico: confident, controlled drawing with the pen, with some tight, rapid shading in parallel strokes, followed by a very painterly application of wash. Reni was attracted to the naturalism of the Carracci while apprenticed to Denys Calvaert, and, after a break with his master, joined the Accademia degli Incamminati in 1594. By the time this drawing was made, his reputation was secure, as he had been chosen, in competition with Bartolomeo Cesi and Lodovico Carracci, to paint the festive decoration for the visit to Bologna of Clement XIV in 1598.

---

[1] D. Stephen Pepper, in Bologna, *Guido Reni,* p. 195, under c. 1598, mentions a drawing in an American private collection which may be connected with the same painting.

Cristofano Allori

(b. Florence 1577; d. Florence 1621)

29 Portrait of Christine of Lorraine, Grand Duchess of Tuscany

Red and black chalks. 328 × 232.

Collections:
David Carritt. Purchased in 1960.

Selected literature:
Sutton, no. 45; Macandrew, no. 784A.

An economical technique, in which two types of chalk were used, has resulted in this memorable image of an authoritative figure. Christine, daughter of Charles III of Lorraine, was born in 1565, and married Ferdinand I de'Medici (1549–1609), Grand Duke of Tuscany, in 1589. She died in 1637. Here she is shown as a widow, probably in her early fifties.

The red chalk has been confined to the flesh, while the black conveys a wider range of textures – hair, eyes, eyebrows, shadows on the flesh and costume. The transparency of the stiff net widow's hood is particularly well conveyed. Allori has rubbed the chalk quite lightly across the grain of the paper, so that the flesh has a vibrant quality, with beautifully modulated shadows. The artist has provided the image of a powerful woman, who gazes directly at the spectator with hooded eyes and firmly set lips. The drawing was probably made in preparation for a portrait; another study of Christine in profile, also in red and black chalks, seems likely to be by Allori, possibly even made at the same sitting.[1] Filippo Baldinucci, who worked at the Medici court, records that Christine did not like sitting for portraits: when, as a new bride, she was painted by Santi di Tito, she would allow the artist no more than half an hour with her.[2] Other early sources[3] suggest that Christine actively disliked Allori, having favoured Lodovico Cigoli as her court painter.

Some documentary references suggest that Allori could have painted a portrait of Christine before 1618, for which this drawing might have been preparatory. He was certainly working on a large portrait in 1620. Her likeness is well known from such works as Scipio Pulzone's portrait of 1590 and a much later full-length by Sustermans.[4]

---

[1] Courtauld Institute of Art, London (Witt Collection, no. 3960).
[2] Baldinucci, II, p. 544; VII, p. 21.
[3] Pizzorusso, p. 11.
[4] Langedijk, nos. 31.19, 31.21.

Ottavio Leoni

(b. Rome 1587; d. Rome 1630)

30   Portrait of a Princess Peretti

Black and white chalks on grey paper. 193 × 155.

Inscribed by the artist:
    S. Ana Maria 1611. Inscribed in a different hand: *Princip.a Peretti.*

Collections:
    Jean-Denis Lempereur (L. 1740). Purchased in 1948 (Hope Collection).

Selected literature:
    Parker, II, no. 879.

Ottavio Leoni made a speciality of these small scale, intimate portraits of high-ranking Roman nobles. Some are in black, red and white chalks on blue paper, while in others a monochrome technique is used, giving a more gentle and subdued effect, as here. The drawing is inscribed by the artist on the left, with the name of the sitter and the date, while the additional identification is in a later hand, possibly that of Ippolito Leoni, the artist's son.[1] The Peretti family, which counted Sixtus V as a member, died out in the mid-seventeenth century. The drawing is made with a very light, deft touch, in soft, feathery strokes. Leoni has adopted the device of having his sitter read a book, which accounts for her pleased and alert expression, but also enables her to be shown modestly lowering her gaze.

Leoni also painted some portraits – he was given the title of Knight of the Order of Christ by Gregory XV (1621–23) in gratitude for one – and a few altar-pieces. However, he is best known for his drawn portraits, the majority of which date from 1614 onwards, when he began to give them serial numbers. He became Principe of the Academy of St Luke in that year, which may have stimulated him to begin a series of portrait drawings of artists; those, and a later series of artists, writers and scientists begun in 1621, were especially celebrated, and many were engraved by Leoni himself.[2] Around four hundred of the artist's drawn portraits were collected by Prince Borghese, and Mariette viewed them when they were sold in Paris in 1747 on the death of their last owner, M. d'Aubigny. Parker suggests that this drawing, and others which bear Lempereur's mark, may have come from the Borghese collections.

---

[1] Spike, p. 15.
[2] Bartsch, XVII, pp. 246–59.

Gian Lorenzo Bernini

(b. Naples 1598; d. Rome 1680)

31   Portrait of the Artist

Black and red chalks with traces of white.
275 × 215.

Collections:
    William Rogers (L. 624); William Young
Ottley. Purchased in 1944 (Hope Collection).

Selected literature:
    Parker, II, no. 792; Wittkower; Sutherland
Harris, no. 23.

Highly finished portrait drawings made as independent works of art were popular in seventeenth century Rome (see also no. 30). This type of drawing, in black, red and white chalks, where the natural buff tone of the paper is given a value as a flesh tone, had earlier been explored by the Carracci, and Bernini must have been stimulated by Annibale's portrait drawings in particular. The careful attention to the modelling of the features, and the examination of light and shade, suggest a sculptor's awareness of form.

The drawing was first identified as a self-portrait by Wittkower, but some scholars, notably Sutherland Harris, have not been convinced. The directness of the gaze is typical of a self-portrait; the tousled hair and the suggestion of a loose shirt give an air of spontaneity and intimacy to the drawing, which is also characteristic of Bernini's known self-portraits (as in a late example at Windsor[1]). His appearance as a young man is known through a portrait drawing of 1622 by Ottavio Leoni,[2] part of a series of portraits of great artists, scientists and writers. There, Bernini is a rather elegant, refined figure, with the typically aloof yet gentle air shared by Leoni's figures. The same young sitter appears in a painted self-portrait of the early 1620s in the Borghese Gallery, Rome, this time as a romantic, intense figure. The model in the Ashmolean drawing is remarkably like the Bernini of the authenticated likenesses, but in a sober, serious mood, probably drawn in the mid-1620s. A drawing in the Gabinetto Nazionale delle Stampe, Rome, is clearly based on the Ashmolean work, and may be an autograph replica.[3]

[1] Blunt & Cooke, no. 54.
[2] Bibliotheca Marucelliana, Florence; Kruft, p. 451.
[3] Catelli Isola, no. 49.

Pier Francesco Mola

(b. Coldrerio 1612; d. Rome 1666)

32 Caricature: Composition of Eight Figures

Pen and brush in brown ink. 183 × 264.

Collections:
    Francis Douce, by whom bequeathed
in 1834.

Selected literature:
    Parker, II, no. 915; Kahn-Rossi, no. III 112.

A man with a large, bulbous nose and chin is the main protagonist in a group of caricatures by Mola, including two others in the Ashmolean[1]. Here, he stands rather unsteadily, with a pair of crutches on the ground beside him, expounding on a painting or drawing in his hand, in which a nude, seen from behind, either flies through the air, or dives downwards. Before him, a character with an expensive hat and long wig makes obeisance. Behind are five ill-assorted figures, apparently artists (one carries a portfolio, another a palette and brushes, a third a roll of paper), and a sixth observes from a window. All of them are linked to the main figure by cords — those of the artists are, perhaps significantly, tied to his belt, from which dangles a heavy purse. One can infer that this character had a pivotal role in the Roman art market and that he fancied himself as an art critic. However, it is not at all clear who is pulling the strings: the artists may be in thrall to the dealer, but they watch his performance with critical eyes; the crucial string may be held by the figure at the window.

The sixth figure can in fact be identified with Mola himself, while the main protagonist is Mola's close friend, Nicolo Simonelli, a merchant and administrator who acted as intermediary for various artists and potential clients. The artist and Simonelli appear together in several caricatures, sometimes with explanatory inscriptions. These pen and wash drawings are informal, even personal works, made for a circle of friends for amusement or wry recognition. They have no public role; if anything, they must have provided relief from the financial cares and artistic frustrations which dogged Mola's official career. Caricature was becoming a distinctive genre in seventeenth century Rome: the Carracci and their pupils had popularized it, and artists as diverse as Bernini and Guercino explored its possibilities.

---

[1] Parker, II, nos. 914 and 915A.

Mattia Preti, called Il Cavaliere Calabrese

(b. Taverna 1613; d. La Valletta 1699)

33 Study for a Knight of Malta

Red chalk. 391 × 254 (irregular).

Collections:
    Jonathan Richardson, Junior (L. 2170);
Sir Joshua Reynolds (L. 2364); Uvedale Price.
Purchased in 1955.

Selected literature:
    Parker, II, no. 928*; Macandrew, no. 928A;
Corace, p. 102.

Preti made this magnificent study in preparation for the major commission of the decoration of the church of S. Giovanni in Valletta, Malta. He worked on the vault of the nave between 1661 and 1666, where the fresco decoration consists of eighteen scenes from the life of St John the Baptist, and, flanking the oval windows at the springing of the vault, twenty-four figures of saints, martyrs and heroes of the Order of the Knights of St John. These large scale figures witness and react to the sacred narrative above. This study is for the figure of St Nicasius, who is situated on the right of the window beneath *The Baptist presenting Christ to the People*. In the fresco, he holds a martyr's palm, and a lance, and (judging from a photograph) his right foot rests on the turbaned head of a defeated Turk.

The study is one of drapery and armour, as seen in strong light on a steeply foreshortened figure. Preti took care to stress the metallic sheen of the armour, and to distinguish its hard edges from the soft, heavy folds of the drapery. The beauty of Preti's handling of the red chalk recalls some aspects of the work of Guercino, an artist he greatly admired. The saint is a typically Baroque figure, expansive and energetic. He leans back, looking upwards, while his right leg thrusts forward into space, in a casual but assertive pose. Preti was well versed in this confident Baroque language, thanks to his close acquaintance with the work of Domenichino and Lanfranco early in his career.

The artist made intensive preparations for this demanding project; he was a draughtsman of great concentration, who would revise and improve his ideas as he worked. In this case, the drawing is very close to the final figure in the fresco. A large group of Preti's drawings for S. Giovanni survives;[1] indeed, about one third of his identifiable graphic work is connected with the S. Giovanni frescoes. Preti was himself received as a Knight of Grace into the Order in 1661, and spent the remainder of his career in Malta.

---

[1] Including two other studies in the Ashmolean; Macandrew, nos. 928B and 928C.

Ciro Ferri

(b. Rome 1634; d. Rome 1689)

34   The Virgin and Child adored

Brush drawing in brown ink, heightened with body-colour, over black chalk. 350 × 478.

Collections:
> Francis Douce, by whom bequeathed in 1834.

Selected literature:
> Parker, II, no. 845; Davis, p. 144.

Ciro Ferri was one of the best of Pietro da Cortona's assistants, and enjoyed the patronage of Ferdinand II de'Medici after having completed his master's fresco decoration in the Palazzo Pitti, and, with his reputation as the natural successor to Cortona, went on to complete various other projects in Rome after the latter's death in 1669. Ferri also gained commissions in his own right, having become a member of the Academy of St Luke in 1657; in his later career, with typical Baroque versatility, he gave greater attention to designs for architecture and sculpture.

His talents as a gifted and inventive draughtsman are well illustrated by this highly finished drawing, made for the engraver. Ferri provided a large number of such drawings as individual works for reproduction, or for book illustrations (such as for a papal missal for Alexander VII in 1662), to be engraved notably by Flemish or French specialists like François Spierre, Cornelis Bloemaert or Charles de la Haye. La Haye engraved this design, probably in the mid-1660s,[1] and the inscription on the print identifies the saints as St Catherine of Alexandria (with her attribute of the wheel), St Martina (carrying lilies), St Dorothy (identifiable by her basket of fruit and flowers), and St Agnes (with her attribute of a lamb). All four saints were early Christian virgin martyrs, so that the vista of ancient Roman buildings is particularly appropriate. The asymmetrical composition, with the figures set in rhythmical motion in a stage-like foreground, ultimately derives from Veronesian models as adapted by Cortona. Davis has identified a drawing in the Musée du Louvre as a preparatory study for the Ashmolean work.[2]

---

[1] Le Blanc, II, p. 344, no. 4.
[2] Davis, no. 520, pl. 67; Briganti, p. 301.

Pier Leone Ghezzi

(b. Rome 1674; d. Rome 1755)

35 Countess Falzacappa

Pen and brown ink. 251 × 170.

Collections:
    Pico Cellini; William M. Milliken.
Purchased (Blakiston Fund) in 1976, with the aid
of the Friends of the Ashmolean.

Selected literature:
    Garlick, no. 6; Macandrew, no. 1004A.

Ghezzi is best known today for his caricatures of Roman high society and of Grand Tourists and members of the French Academy, most of which date from the late 1730s onwards. He also had antiquarian and archaeological interests, as did many of those he portrayed, while he acted as dealer, restorer, engraver and leader of fashion amongst other things. In his own day, Ghezzi had a high reputation as a portraitist and history painter: he became Pittore di Corte, or painter to the Pope, in 1708, with a wide range of duties including the charge of the papal tapestry and mosaic factories. The patronage of the Albani family was important to his career, especially that of Clement XI (1700–1721) and of the influential Cardinal Annibale Albani.

This sheet is one of the rare examples of Ghezzi's portrait drawings. A finely dressed lady, with a fan and fur muff, is sensitively portrayed; behind her stands the less restrained figure of a nun, who stares at the spectator, and, on the left, the figure in profile of a manservant, whose features and expression anticipate the later caricatures. Ghezzi used an engraver's technique of shading with close parallel lines, cross-hatching and stippled dots. Two clearly related drawings are known,[1] which are also informal portraits, apparently of members of the same family. One shows two small boys doing their lessons at a table, identified by inscriptions as Serafino and Francesco Falzacappa. The other shows an older woman seated in a chair, who, it is assumed, would be their grandmother. The group of drawings probably date from 1710 or soon after.

Ghezzi certainly had a later connexion with the Falzacappa family, for he was commissioned by them to paint an altar-piece of *The Madonna and Child with St Joseph and the Blessed Felix* (beatified by Clement XI in 1712) for the church of S. Giuseppe in Tarquinia, Viterbo, possibly around 1720.[2]

---

[1] Sold with no. 35 at Sotheby's, London, 21 March 1974, nos. 111 and 112 respectively; the latter was resold at Sotheby's, Florence, 7 April 1976, no. 156.
[2] Lo Bianco, no. 32.

Giambattista Piazzetta

(b. Pietrarosa 1682; d. Venice 1754)

36   Head of a Youth

Black and white chalks on brownish paper.
315 × 299.

Collections:
>   purchased in 1934.

Selected literature:
>   Parker, II, no. 1034; Parker (1958), no. 81;
Sutton, no. 63; Garlick, no. 12; Mariuz, no. D20;
Knox (1983), no. 55.

This beautiful study of a young boy – sometimes called a young ensign – belongs to a large group of drawings which Piazzetta made as independent works of art for the collector. The drawings are, essentially, of expressive heads, many of young men and women – unlike Tiepolo's series of heads of older men (see no. 38) – and occasionally in groups of two or even three. By contrast with Tiepolo's rapid pen and wash drawings, Piazzetta's studies are careful and elaborate. By the 1740s, they were attracting the attention of engravers, and many were reproduced in engravings and mezzotints. These *têtes de caractère* have been compared in achievement with the pastels of Rosalba Carriera.

A warm-toned brown paper was chosen for this drawing, and it remains exposed to convey the lighter parts of the flesh, while some white chalk is used very sparingly where the light hits the face beneath the cap. The black chalk was first rubbed gently (and probably moistened) to create a soft grey film of shadow, which was then worked over, building up a marvellous tonal range, and creating a variety of textures. The position of the tassel was altered in the process. The same models recur in Piazzetta's drawings, and he may well have posed members of his family – here, Knox has suggested, his son, Giacomo, giving a date of *c*. 1743 for the drawing.

Piazzetta was a slow and careful worker by nature: in his paintings, the figures have a solidity of form and intensity of expression which result equally from his masterly, deliberate handling of paint, and from his close attention to the psychology of his protagonists. The same artistic and human interests are seen in these finished drawings, which are absolutely suited to his temperament. Piazzetta's sojourn in Bologna as a youth was crucial to his artistic formation: he assimilated the Bolognese tradition of good draughtsmanship based on sustained practice and observation. In Venice he ran an important 'Scuola del nudo', a life drawing class frequented by the young Tiepolo, and with his reputation as an excellent teacher and draughtsman, he became the first Direttore of the new Venetian Academy in 1750.

Giovanni Battista Tiepolo

(b. Venice 1696; d. Madrid 1770)

37 Head of an old bearded Man

Red chalk, touched with white, on grey-blue paper. 260 × 180 (irregular).

Collections:
Johann Dominik Bossi; Maria Beyerlen; Dr Hans Wendland. Purchased in 1934.

Selected literature:
Parker, II, no. 1081; Parker (1958), no. 64; Knox (1980), no. M.608.

Tiepolo made this confident, vigorous study for one of the figures in the *Miracle of St. Anthony of Padua*, an altar-piece commissioned for the parish church at Mirano, and painted probably in the late 1750s.[1] Red chalk on blue paper was a favourite combination of Giambattista's for preparatory studies of heads, hands and details of costume. The white chalk is applied in delicate touches, conveying both the fall of light on the features, and the texture of the old man's beard. While one eye is in shadow, the other is brilliantly drawn, with a couple of touches of white used to dynamic effect. The boldness of the red strokes against the grain of the paper, together with the light dabs of white, add a sense of vibrancy and luminosity to the drawing. This is entirely appropriate for the drawing's expressive purpose, as a study of the awe and reverence of this humble figure witnessing a miraculous event.

Enough of Giambattista's preparatory work for the altar-piece survives – an oil-sketch, pen and ink compositional studies, and chalk drawings of details – to illustrate how carefully he planned the commission. However, the commission came at a very busy time – these are the years of the fresco decoration of the Villa Valmarana, of major religious commissions for the Duomo at Este, and the Oratorio at Udine - and Giambattista relied on his chief assistant and collaborator, Domenico, for the execution of the Mirano altar-piece to the master's detailed designs.

---

[1] Morassi (1962), p. 29, pl. 132.

38 Head of a bearded Man in a fur Cap

Pen and brown ink and brown wash over black chalk. 247 × 196.

Collections:

the convent of the Sommaschi, Santa Maria della Salute, Venice; Conte Leopoldo Cicognara; Antonio Canova; Monsignor G. B. Sartori-Canova; Francesco Pesaro; Edward Cheney; Col. Alfred Capel Cure; Richard Owen; Alan D. Pilkington, by whom bequeathed in memory of his wife, Florence Mary, in 1973.

Selected literature:

Macandrew, no. 1086D.

This imposing study was once part of an album of drawings which Giambattista left for safe keeping with his son, Giuseppe Maria, a priest at the Sommaschi convent of Santa Maria della Salute, Venice, before his departure for Madrid with his other sons, Domenico and Lorenzo, in late March, 1762. There were ninety-three studies of heads in the album, together with nearly seventy explorations of the theme of the Holy Family. After his return from Spain upon his father's death, Domenico made use of some of the head studies in that album, as they appear in a collection of etchings of fanciful and exotic male heads, mostly after Giambattista, the *Raccolta di Teste*, etched *c.* 1773, and published in memory of his father.

Tiepolo made shorthand notations first on the page, using black chalk; another idea for a similar head is sketched briefly on the right. The artist brushed on light and dark washes over the chalk in a most economical fashion, but to wonderful effect, creating not only a striking study of light and shade, but also a powerfully expressive head. Exotically dressed characters such as this one – notice the cameo-like gem decorating his fur hat – appear in Giambattista's paintings throughout his career, generally as colourful spectators in a variety of subjects, from biblical to classical. They are central characters in the master's more intimate works in mid-career, his etchings of the *Capricci* and the *Scherzi di fantasia*.

Tiepolo's series of heads are permutations on one subject, that of elderly, foreign men: a variety of moods and physiognomy is explored, in drawings ranging from witty near-caricatures to sober depictions of grandly majestic characters with the air of Old Testament patriarchs. It was to this aspect of Giambattista's inventiveness that Francesco Algarotti referred, when he wrote of his friend's pungent imagination, and likened him to Salvator Rosa and Giovanni Benedetto Castiglione.[1] Anton Maria Zanetti the Elder invoked the tradition of Castiglione and Rembrandt as inventive graphic artists with whom Tiepolo could compare in taste and virtuosity.[2]

[1] Algarotti, p. 22.
[2] in a letter of 1757 to P.-J. Mariette; Bacou (1967), no. 318.

Giovanni Antonio Canal, called Canaletto

(b. Venice 1697; d. Venice 1768)

39 An Island in the Lagoon

Pen and brown ink with grey wash over ruled pencil lines. 200 × 279.

Collections:

Otto Gutekunst. Presented by Mrs Otto Gutekunst in memory of her husband in 1947.

Selected literature:

Parker, II, no. 980; Parker (1958), no. 85; Sutton, no. 67; Garlick, no. 1; Constable & Links, no. 654; Bettagno (1982), no. 62; Baetjer and Links, no. 108.

In this superb finished drawing, Canaletto made masterly use of grey washes to evoke the soft, hazy atmosphere of the Venetian lagoon, where the glare of the sun striking on boats and buildings can have an almost blinding effect. The white paper conveys this sense of bright, diffused light, while the sharpened details outlined thinly in brown calligraphic strokes add to the vibrancy of the drawing. The church and monastery of S. Michele in Isola are viewed from the north; beyond the cemetery island, the Fondamente Nuove can be seen, with the church of S. Francesco della Vigna and, in the distance, the dome (but not the campanile) of S. Pietro di Castello. The drawing was certainly made for its own sake, and probably dates from the early 1740s.

This was obviously a composition Canaletto liked, as a number of variations by the artist are known. He made a pen and ink drawing around the same time, with considerable alterations in detail, for his principal patron, the merchant Joseph Smith (c. 1674–1770), who became British Consul at Venice in 1744; this drawing is now in the Royal Collection at Windsor.[1] Versions and copies of the Windsor and Ashmolean drawings are known. On his second trip to England, Canaletto painted the same view as part of a decorative scheme of six pictures (the other five were capricci, and one is dated 1754), probably commissioned by the third Baron King for Ockham Place, Surrey.[2] Much later, the design was published by Joseph Wagner in a series of six etchings after Canaletto, *Sei Villaggi Campestri*, probably in 1760–65.[3] The Ashmolean drawing seems to have been the model for Wagner's etching.

---

[1] Constable & Links, no. 653.
[2] See Constable & Links, nos. 367, 473–78 and 504.
[3] Pignatti (1969), no. 4, fig. 25.

Francesco Guardi

(b. Venice 1712; d. Venice 1793)

40   The Villa Loredan at Paese

Pen and brown ink with grey wash over preliminary indications in black chalk. 321 × 535.

Inscribed in black ink:

View of the Seat of S. E. Loredano at Paese near Treviso at present in the possession of John Strange Esqr N.B. grass ground within the Fence; without the post road from Treviso to Bassan.

Collections:
purchased in 1950.

Selected literature:
Byam Shaw (1951), under no. 30; Parker, II, no. 1015; Parker (1958), no. 115; Sutton, no. 70; Morassi, *Disegni*, no. 423.

Guardi's breezy panoramic view is both a record of this imposing Palladian-style villa, taken from the north, and a portrayal of the fashionably dressed Venetians who enjoyed their annual *villeggiatura* at such country retreats. The inscription on the drawing, which identifies the now destroyed villa, is in the hand of John Strange (1732–1799), a diplomat and antiquarian who was British Resident at Venice from 1773 to 1788. He was an important patron and collector of Francesco Guardi. The Villa Loredan was sold by the Conte Gerolamo Antonio Loredan to the Marchese Giuseppe de Canonicis some time before 1779; Strange may have leased it as a summer retreat. Another highly finished drawing in the Ashmolean by Guardi,[1] shows a view from one of the back windows at the villa, suggesting that the artist was a welcome visitor there.

The drawing corresponds very closely to a painting by Guardi formerly in the Rothermere Collection,[2] which is one of a set of four views once owned by Strange, and probably commissioned by him.[3] The other views show the garden façade of the Villa Loredan, with an artist sketching in the foreground; the nearby Villa del Timpano Arcuato, again with an extensive surrounding view; and the gardens of the Palazzo Contarini dal Zaffo in Venice. The style of the pictures, and the costume of the little figures, make a date of the very late 1770s likely, possibly 1778, when Guardi had made a rare visit to the mainland to view family property at Piano, north of Treviso.

While two elaborate preparatory drawings are known for the ex-Rothermere picture,[4] Guardi seems to have made this drawing as a *ricordo* rather than as a preliminary study. Strange's explanatory inscription, with its emphasis on the grass inside the gates, and the villa's location on the main road, could have been intended for an English acquaintance who had seen neither the villa nor the painting.

[1] Parker, II, no. 1016.
[2] Sold Christie's, London, 8 December 1989, no. 114.
[3] Morassi, *Dipinti*, nos. 680–83.
[4] Morassi, *Disegni*, nos. 421–22.

View of the Seat of S.E. Loredano at Paese near Treviso at present in the possession of John Strange Esq.r — N.B. grass ground within the fence; without the post road from Treviso to Bassano.

Giovanni Battista Piranesi

(b. Mozano di Mestre 1720; d. Rome 1788)

41   An architectural Fantasy

Pen and ink with brown wash over red chalk.
365 × 505.

Inscribed (signed?):
Piranesi.

Collections:
Earl of Abingdon. Purchased in 1935
(Sadler Fund).

Selected literature:
Thomas, no. 37; Parker, II, no. 1039;
Salamon, no. 189; Wilton-Ely, no. 47; Bettagno
(1978), no. 33.

This scene of extravagant architecture, boldly and lavishly executed, is utterly characteristic of Piranesi's maturity. By the mid-1750s, when the drawing was made, he had produced the first edition of the *Invenzioni capric. di carceri* (c. 1745–50), a series of brooding images of ancient labyrinthine prisons, and the *Opere varie* of c. 1750, a collection of etchings inspired by his study of the architecture of Imperial Rome. Piranesi's ambitious *Antichità romane*, published in four volumes in 1756, helped to establish his reputation as an archaeologist and antiquarian scholar.

The drawing creates a magnificent, complex building which evokes the grandeur of the antique, not just in terms of the Roman engineering skills Piranesi so admired, but equally in terms of the Imperial richness of ornament of capitals, spandrels, niches, urns and candelabra, which stimulated his own designs. The gigantic scale of the architecture, and the suggestion of light pouring through domed spaces, is reminiscent of some of the great Roman basilicas, from St Peter's to S. Giovanni in Laterano, which Piranesi studied for his *Vedute di Roma*, published from c. 1748 to the 1770s. The organization of space in this imaginary edifice recalls the heritage of Baroque stage design, from the Bibiena family's vast receding structures set at angles to each other, to Filippo Juvarra's spirited spatial constructions. Of Piranesi's many admirers and imitators, Charles Michel-Ange Challe was perhaps most influenced by this sort of design. However, Piranesi's bold and painterly execution is unrivalled, particularly in its use of flourishes of dark ink to denote figures in movement, and to give depth and form to a variety of motifs.

Giovanni Domenico Tiepolo

(b. Venice 1727; d. Venice 1804)

42 Studies of a Dog

Pen with brown wash over black chalk.
208 × 268.

Collections:
    purchased in 1937.

Selected literature:
    Parker, II, no. 1100; Parker (1958), no. 99;
Byam Shaw (1962), p. 45.

These studies of a dog resembling a retriever were certainly made from life, with the artist quickly sketching the animal in black chalk as it changed position. Domenico then worked up the sketches, going over them with pen, ink, and different shades of wash; he also brushed the wash over the page so as to provide a neutral, though not uniform, setting, but principally to allow the white of the paper to stand out strongly as a light-filled area. Domenico may have begun with the study of a seated dog, as he twice changed his mind about the placing of the head; he then began a second study beside it, in the centre of the page (some black chalk indications of the hind quarters of a dog are visible), but rejected this in favour of a more deliberate *placement* of the studies. Life studies of animals are rare in Domenico's *oeuvre*: he generally relied on printed sources, such as Stefano della Bella's etchings, for inspiration. Pen and ink was Domenico's preferred drawing technique, and his spirited, lavish handling of the medium contrasts sharply with Giambattista's restraint.

A variety of dogs appear in paintings by Domenico and his father, and Domenico sometimes used the same details of animals in more than one work, so that these studies could have been made with a painting in mind. However, Domenico was a prolific draughtsman, and, even more than his father, he made use of drawing and etching for the creative exploration of various themes, religious and secular – we know of several series of drawings which are signed and probably intended for the collector. His many drawings of dogs and other animals provided him with a repertoire of motifs, and were doubtless viewed as attractive sheets in their own right.

Domenico Tiepolo

43 Landscape with a Dog and a Farm Cart

Pen with brown wash over black chalk.
351 × 290.

Inscribed:
    95.

Collections:
    purchased in 1935.

Selected literature:
    Parker, II, no. 1097; Byam Shaw (1962), p. 59; Gealt and Vetrocq, no. 13.

One of Domenico's favourite mongrel dogs is shown in an attractive mountainous landscape in this mutilated half of a larger composition. The location of the other half is unknown, but an old photograph shows the drawing in 1921, before the offensive right hand side was cut away (fig. 1). The drawing was part of the *Divertimento per li regazzi*, a series of one hundred and four drawings (including the title page) made by Domenico in his old age, most likely around 1800. The set was still intact after its initial sale in 1920, but the drawings were sold and dispersed after being exhibited in Paris in 1921.

Domenico illustrated the life and adventures of Punchinello, exploring all the vices and quirks of character of this Commedia dell'Arte anti-hero. Punchinello is lecherous, lazy, dishonest, a glutton, a jester, and a buffoon; his picaresque escapades include travels in the East, imprisonment, employment at the circus, and a career as a history painter. The series displays Domenico's sharp wit and sense of humour: all shades of humour are represented, from the slapstick and lavatorial to some delightful parodies and well aimed satire. This is Domenico's final and most personal series, and best epitomizes his distinctive genius. All manner of recollections of earlier compositions and motifs are blended (here, Domenico re-uses a study of some buildings in Udine, probably made *c.* 1759) to create a fresh and vivacious set of variations on the Punchinello theme.

As a keen collector of prints, Domenico would have known of earlier treatments of Punchinello's character in the work of Callot and Ghezzi; other artists such as Alessandro Magnasco, or, more to the point, Giambattista Tiepolo, had depicted this burlesque figure. Domenico's most important exploration of the subject prior to the *Divertimento* had again been a personal one: around 1793 he had decorated in fresco a room of the family villa at Zianigo with playful Punchinello scenes (the frescoes are now in the Ca'Rezzonico, Venice).

Fig. 1. Domenico Tiepolo, *Landscape*

Francisco Goya

(b. Fuente de Todos 1746; d. Bordeaux 1828)

44 Naked Savage about to cudgel another

Brush drawing in sepia and grey wash.
207 × 141.

Collections:

    Paul Lebas; Percy Moore Turner; Francis Falconer Madan, by whom bequeathed in 1962.

Selected literature:

    Gassier & Wilson, no. 1478; Gassier, no. F57; Guillaud (1979), no. 175; Hofmann (1980–81), no. 165; Pérez Sánchcz, no. 151.

Goya used the brush and several shades of wash for this study of a murderous group of two men, naked but for some animal skins. The violence of the subject is echoed in the fierce handling of the medium. It has been called *Samson and the Philistine*, or *Cain and Abel*, but Goya did not necessarily have a particular subject in mind, other than the ubiquity of aggression. Around the same time, Goya made a profound exploration of human brutality in his *Disasters of War* etchings, begun *c.* 1810, with the final plates dating from 1815–20, while some small pictures of the 1808–14 period[1] also illustrate savage themes of murder, torture and rape.

The drawing comes from an album of brush and sepia ink studies, one of eight albums which the artist planned and compiled as coherent sequences. This album contains drawings spanning the years 1812–23, with the majority of them made in 1815–20. It was broken up, and many drawings sold, in the 1840s by Goya's son Javier, who was in financial difficulties. The subjects include scenes of imprisonment, torture and death; there are violent and grotesque subjects, scenes of duelling and hunting, and also some everyday scenes of crowds at the Casa del Campo (near where Goya bought his house, the Quinta del Sordo, in 1819). This sheet and the dynamic drawing which followed it in the album, *Man holding back a horse*[2], seem rather different in style from the others: the possibility that they were drawn somewhat earlier, and added to this album by Goya, should not be excluded.

[1] Gassier & Wilson, nos. 916–31.
[2] Gassier, no. F58.

45   Benjamin taking Leave of his Father

Pen and black ink over outline of brown ink, touched in places with body-colour by a later hand. 230 in diameter.

Collections:

C. M. Metz; Francis Douce, by whom bequeathed in 1834.

Selected literature:

Popham (1931), no. 5; Parker, I, no. 8; Lloyd (1982), no. 25.

The drawing represents Benjamin, the youngest son of Jacob, taking leave of his father, who is seated on the left, while his elder brothers are shown standing in the foreground on the right (Genesis 43. 1–15).

There are four related drawings from the series of circular designs illustrating the life of Joseph for stained glass, although in comparison with the present sheet these have the appearance of being copies rather than originals.[1] Two glass roundels[2] as well as six circular paintings[3] probably derived from the drawings exist, but none of these includes the subject of the present drawing.

A clearly recognisable group of drawings has been established as by the hand of an artist working after or in the style of Hugo van der Goes. On the basis of two sheets illustrating the life of Tobit, which also connect with existing glass roundels,[4] the artist is known as the Master of the Story of Tobit, who, it has been surmised, was a designer for stained glass working in the Netherlands during the last quarter of the fifteenth century.

[1] Oxford; Parker, I, nos. 9–10, and Bayonne and Berlin; Popham (1931), pp. 75, 122.
[2] Musée des Hospices Civils, Bruges and formerly in the Oppenheimer collection.
[3] Berlin, New York and Munich; Friedländer, IV, p. 80, pls. 70–71.
[4] Royal Collection, Windsor and Dresden; see Popham (1928), p. 178.

Lucas van Leyden

(b. Leyden 1489/94; d. Leyden 1533)

46 St Jerome

Black chalk, with several lines drawn with the point of the brush in brown and dark washes, and traces of pen and dark ink, heightened with white, the background in blue body-colour.
376 × 281.

Signed with the artist's initial and dated:
1521.
Inscribed in gold:
ST. HIERONEMUS; ABD.

Collections:
William Hartnup. Purchased in 1953.

Selected literature:
Kloek, no. 19; Lloyd (1982), no. 27.

The saint is shown seated at a table, with his right hand resting on a skull, while a crucifix is supported against his shoulder. The artist's now barely legible signature appears to have been cut out at some time and re-inserted upside down. The blue background, recalling portrait miniatures by Hans Holbein the Younger, although certainly old may not be original. The gold inscriptions may have been added at the same time.

In 1521, the year of the drawing, Lucas van Leyden made an engraving of the saint,[1] but since the arrangement is different, it is unlikely that the present drawing was intended as a preparatory study.

In the same year, Dürer visited the Netherlands and became friends with, among other artists, Lucas van Leyden. Apart from executing a silverpoint portrait of the latter in Antwerp,[2] Dürer also produced a painting of *St Jerome*,[3] which, in the introduction of a skull and the motif of the saint's pointing finger, appears to have influenced Lucas, among other Netherlandish artists, in both the present drawing and the engraving of 1521. (These elements were not present in two earlier engravings of *St Jerome* by Lucas.) Unusually highly finished, Lucas van Leyden's drawing was probably done as a work of art in its own right in emulation of the substantial number of such works produced by Dürer during his tour of the Netherlands. The general influence of the German artist both in style and technique is emphasised by the old ascription to Dürer on the present sheet.

---

[1] Bartsch, VII, p. 398, no. 114.
[2] Lille; Winkler, no. 816.
[3] Lisbon; Anzelewsky, no. 162. There are also five elaborate preparatory drawings; Panofsky, nos. 817–21.

Jan Swart

(b. Groningen *c.* 1500; d. Gouda *c.* 1558)

47   The Schoolmaster of Falerii

Pen and black ink with grey wash, over black chalk. 350 × 215 (arched at top).

Collections:
> S. Gautier; Nathaniel Hone (L. 2793); J. F. Keane. Purchased in 1949 (Campbell Dodgson Bequest Fund).

Selected literature:
> Hand, no. 110.

This story exemplifying Roman virtue, rarely represented in art, is recounted by Livy (V, 27), Plutarch (*Camillus*, 10) and Valerius Maximus (VI, 5.1). During a lull in the siege of the Etruscan town of Falerii carried out by the Romans under Camillus in the fourth century BC, a schoolmaster, under the guise of exercising his pupils outside the walls, traitorously leads them into the Roman camp and offers them as hostages. His proposal is contemptuously rejected by Camillus, who orders his soldiers to strip the schoolmaster and tie his hands behind his back. Watched by Camillus and his soldiers (standing before their tents in the background of the present drawing), the master is driven back by his pupils armed with sticks to Falerii, where the inhabitants, overcome by the magnanimity of Camillus, yield to the Romans.

As well as being a painter and printmaker, Swart played an influential role in Gouda as a designer of stained glass windows.

A drawing of the same dimensions and in a similar style, representing the *Justice of Cambyses*,[1] was probably conceived as a pendant to the present sheet, and it is likely that both studies were intended as designs for stained glass. Since it was common practice in the fifteenth and sixteenth centuries to decorate town halls with representations of scenes of justice, it can be surmised that these two examples of ancient justice were destined possibly as part of a series for the windows of a courtroom.

The drawing shows a general stylistic similarity to Swart's woodcuts executed in the late 1520s, but the greater substance of the figures and their freedom of movement suggest a slightly later date of *c.* 1530.

---

[1] Dresden; Baldass, no. 21.

Maerten van Heemskerck

(b. Heemskerk 1498; d. Haarlem 1574)

48 Jonah, seated under the Gourd, contemplates the City of Nineveh

Pen and brown ink, incised with the stylus.
197 × 252.

Signed:
M. Heemskerck inventor 1566.
Inscribed on the *verso*:
van Heemskerck histori van Jonah no. 27.

Collections:
purchased in 1948.

Selected literature:
Lloyd (1982), no. 28.

The subject, taken from the Prophecy of Jonah, 4. 5–6, illustrates the moment when Jonah, having gone out of the city of Nineveh to watch its fate, is seated beside the River Tigris under the gourd, which had miraculously grown up to shade him from the sun and comfort him in his grief. God the Father accompanied by angels appears in the clouds above.

The drawing is a preparatory study for the engraving, in reverse, by Philip Galle, which forms part of a series of four illustrating the story of Jonah.[1] (The preparatory drawings for the other three prints are known.[2]) The subject was popular with the artist and occurs earlier in a painting of 1561[3] and in another engraving by Philip Galle of the following year.[4]

Apart from painting, Van Heemskerck was very active as a designer for prints engraved by a number of different artists, which Karel van Mander said 'filled the entire world with inventions'. Befitting their purpose, his drawings tend to be drawn in an elaborately hatched manner suitable for transference to copper. As a result of his visit to Italy earlier in his life, he was a keen student of antique and Renaissance art and was subsequently in contact with humanist circles at home. His imaginative reconstruction of the city of Nineveh shows something of these interests.

---

[1] Hollstein, VIII, p. 243, no. 271.
[2] Museum of Fine Arts, Boston, Fitzwilliam Museum, Cambridge and formerly the collection of Dr E. Perman, Stockholm.
[3] Hampton Court; White, no. 3.
[4] Hollstein, VIII, p. 245, no. 367.

1566.

M. Heemskerck
jnvento

Pieter Bruegel the Elder

(b. Brueghel *c.* 1525/30; d. Brussels 1569)

49   The Temptation of St Antony

Pen and black ink on brownish (discoloured) paper. 216 × 326.

Inscribed (signed?):
Bruegel 1556.

Collections:
Francis Douce, by whom bequeathed in 1834.

Selected literature:
Parker, I, no. 30; Münz, no. 127; Winner (1975), no. 62; Lloyd (1982), no. 29.

The drawing was reproduced in the same direction in an engraving by Pieter van der Heyden[1] which shows that the sheet has been cut at the bottom. The signature on the drawing does not appear to be by Bruegel, although it may be a copy of an original signature on the missing piece of paper. The drawing has sometimes been regarded as a copy but is now generally accepted as an original.

St Antony the Great was an Egyptian saint, who lived as a hermit for many years in the desert. Like other hermits he suffered from hallucinations which are usually represented in art as temptations either from an assault by demons or from erotic visions. But unlike the latter, Bruegel's composition includes neither demons nor naked women, and the small moneybag (cut from the drawing) is the only insignificant evidence of temptation. The print is inscribed with the title 'Many are the afflictions of the righteous, but the Lord delivereth him out of them all'. Bruegel's interpretation of the subject has been much debated but it appears to be concerned principally with the corruption of the Church and the foolishness of the world, on which the kneeling saint, absorbed in his book, has turned his back.

The present study is among the earliest of four compositions by Bruegel[2] which were engraved and published by Hieronymus Cock in Antwerp, but unlike the others it does not show such a dependance on the work of Hieronymus Bosch, although individual details can be paralleled in the work of the latter. All, however, show the satirical and moralising aspect of the older artist. Bruegel repeated the motif of the two fantastic figures jousting in the left of the foreground in his painting of *The Fight between Carnival and Lent* of 1559.[3]

---

[1] Bastelaer, no. 119.
[2] *Big fish eating little fish* in Vienna, *The ass in the school* in Berlin and *Avaritia* in the British Museum, London; Münz, nos. 128–30.
[3] Vienna; Grossmann, pls. 9–12.

Hendrick Goltzius

(b. Mulbrecht 1558; d. Haarlem 1617)

50   Head of Mercury

Pen and brown ink. 444 × 365.

Signed:

H Goltzius fecit. A°. 1587

Collections:

Rudolf II; Queen Christina of Sweden; Hugh Howard; Mrs E. E. Dodsworth. Purchased in 1954.

Selected literature:

Reznicek, no. 119; Lloyd (1982), no. 31; Hand, no. 54.

This large drawing, dominated by the direct and imposing gaze of Mercury, generally considered to be the inventor of the arts, was executed in 1587, between the time that Goltzius set up as a print publisher in Haarlem in 1582 and his departure in 1590 for a short but thorough tour of Italy. The hatched style of his drawings of these years had been formed by his study of the prints of both Dürer and Lucas van Leyden in connexion with his own work for the medium. Their less flamboyant manner of drawing had, however, been modified by Goltzius's admiration for the virtuoso penwork, with its flourishing swelling lines, of the imperial court artist, Bartholomäus Spranger (1546–1611). Goltzius had been introduced to the latter's drawings by his fellow Haarlem artist, Karel van Mander (1548–1606), who had earlier worked with Spranger in Vienna. (Around the time of this drawing Goltzius, Van Mander and Cornelis van Haarlem (1562–1638) had established an inform-al 'academy' to draw from the life.) This drawing style, which was to char-acterize his work until he abandoned engraving for painting, had only been first seen in the previous year in the drawing of *Marcus Curtius*.[1]

This drawing is one of a number of large studies executed during the decade. It does not connect with any other known work in the artist's *oeuvre*, although the style and scale, as well as the presentation of the bust covered by drapery, are similar to the *Head of a Woman*, signed and now dated 1588 (the last digit was altered, suggesting that the sheet may have been started in either 1580 or 1586).[2] Such exhibitions of virtuosity were probably done as works in their own right to be sold or given away as pre-sentation drawings. They were much admired at the time, emphasised in the present example by its probable ownership by the Emperor Rudolf II in Prague, who died in 1612.

[1] Copenhagen; Reznicek, no. 142
[2] Besançon; Reznicek, no. 360.

51   Study of a Tree

Pen and dark brown ink, brush and water- and body-colours, on blue prepared paper. 424 × 302.

Signed with monogram.

Collections:
Francis Falconer Madan, by whom bequeathed in 1962.

Selected literature:
Reznicek, no. 410; Lloyd (1982), no. 32; Hand, no. 62.

Unique in Goltzius's existing *oeuvre*, this large and beautiful study of a tree was probably drawn about 1600. Clearly done from nature, it was probably executed about the same time and in the same locality as the two existing studies of groups of trees in the woods around Haarlem, which were also executed in coloured washes on blue prepared paper.[1] (The beauty of the Haarlem woods, which were also studied by other artists, was celebrated in a contemporary poem by Karel van Mander in *Lofdicht op Haarlem*, published in 1596.) These nature studies led on after the turn of the century to a more extensive exploration of realistic landscape by Goltzius and other Haarlem artists.

The preoccupation with colour in the various studies of trees, which foreshadows the artist's interest in taking up painting around 1600, can be paralleled with other works of the period, notably the four small undated landscapes in woodcut, printed both on blue paper heightened with white body-colour and in chiaroscuro.[2] In both his drawn and printed landscapes in colour, Goltzius was undoubtedly influenced by Venetian woodcuts after Titian, promoted as exemplars for young artists by Karel van Mander in his treatise, *Het Schilderboek* (Haarlem, 1604). In his studies of trees, it has been suggested that Goltzius may also have seen similar works by Federico Barocci *(c.* 1535–1612), who, apart from the few sheets existing today, left behind in his studio at Urbino a large number of landscape studies.

Whether there were originally other similar studies of trees, or whether the present study was modified according to need, a similar massive tree trunk is employed by Goltzius as the central background feature supporting the figure or figures in such works as the highly finished drawing on parchment of *Venus, Bacchus, Ceres and Cupid* of 1593[3] and the engraved portrait of *Frederik de Vries* of 1597.[4] A similar tree recurs in the background of the very large drawing of the *Birth of Adonis*, dated 1603.[5]

---

[1] Hamburg and Fondation Custodia, Paris; Reznicek, nos. 397 and 402.
[2] Hollstein, VIII, p. 127, nos. 378–81
[3] British Museum, London; Reznicek, no. 129.
[4] Hollstein, VIII, p. 71, no. 190.
[5] Amsterdam; Reznicek, no. 111.

Jacques de Gheyn the Younger

(b. Antwerp 1565; d. The Hague 1629)

52 Gipsy Woman and Child

Pen and brown ink on grey paper. 187 × 159.

Collections:
Dr Edward Peart (L. 891); Francis Douce, by whom bequeathed in 1834.

Selected literature:
Parker, I, no. 38; Van Regteren Altena (1983), no. 536; Meij, no. 60.

This sharply observed study of a woman and child seated on the ground seen from the back, which can be seen as a precursor of Rembrandt's numerous studies of women and children, belongs to a group of drawings of gipsies which found their final expression in a large engraving by De Gheyn of *The Fortune Teller*.[1] (The seated gipsy leaning against the old fortune teller on the right of the print is not dissimilar to that in the drawing.) The woman is dressed in a characteristic gipsy costume and the basket she holds on her knee may well be for sale; gipsies were traditionally associated with the manufacture and sale of basket, copper and woodwork. Although at first accepted in the Netherlands as well as throughout Western Europe, gipsies came to be regarded as undesirable; in 1595 a special edict was issued by the States of Holland forbidding them from begging. But they, and particularly their language, were the subject of study at Leiden University and it has been suggested that De Gheyn's acquaintance with members of the university may have encouraged his interest in the Romany people.

None of the works is dated, but they may have been executed towards the end of the first decade of the seventeenth century, after De Gheyn's move to The Hague in 1603, possibly at the same time that he was engaged in studies of the somewhat related subject of witches. But, unlike his interest in the latter which follows a tradition going back to the previous century, the studies of gipsies exemplify the new examination of the surrounding world. His penwork follows the general style of engravers, seen also in the earlier work of Goltzius, in whose studio De Gheyn worked as an engraver around 1585, but in his drawings he develops a freedom and expressiveness far beyond the capability of the burin.

[1] Hollstein, VII, p. 126, no. 105.

53 Neptune

Pen and brown ink heightened with body-colour, on brownish paper. 231 × 279.

Signed and dated:
1610 IDG.in.

Collections:
Francis Douce, by whom bequeathed in 1834.

Selected literature:
Parker, I, no. 40; Van Regteren Altena (1983), no. 121.

Neptune, the god who ruled the sea, is here depicted as an old man with a long beard. His head-dress is made up of shells and his waist is encircled by a large fish. As has been pointed out, his appearance bears some resemblance to Michelangelo's sculpture of *Moses* in S. Pietro in Vincoli in Rome. On the right a youth is shown blowing a conch, while the foreground is filled with large shells. Shells are used as an even more prominent foreground motif in an otherwise unrelated painting of *Neptune with Amphitrite and Cupid*,[1] probably made about the same time or shortly before, suggesting that it may have been commissioned by one of the contemporary collectors of shells. (The artist himself owned a collection of rare shells.)

Executed while De Gheyn was living in The Hague, this drawing is one of the few in the artist's *oeuvre* devoted to mythological subjects. Its purpose is not known, but over a decade later in the 1620s, De Gheyn was commissioned by the Stadholder, Prince Maurice, to design a garden and pavilion or grotto on the *Buitenhof* next to his residence at The Hague. Included in the scheme of decoration was a large sculpted relief of Neptune seated among shells and fishes, for which two preparatory drawings still exist.[2] Although the final form of the sculpture was very different, the present drawing may have served as a starting point.

---

[1] Cologne; Van Regteren Altena (1983), no. 5.
[2] Pierpont Morgan Library, New York and the British Museum, London; Van Regteren Altena (1983), nos. 162–63.

Jan Brueghel the Elder

(b. Brussels 1568; d. Antwerp 1625)

54 Landscape

Brush drawing in brown and blue washes.
256 × 399.

Inscribed on the *verso*:
> *dees thien teeckeninghen principalen van Johannes brueghel ofte franweedn breughel costen tesamen fx guldens in comptant ghelt.*

Collections:
> purchased in 1948.

Selected literature:
> Lloyd (1982), no. 36.

The inscription on the back of the sheet, which supports the attribution to Jan Brueghel the Elder, suggests that it was part of a group of ten drawings, characterized as being 'important', an assessment which is not inconsistent with the undoubted quality of the present example. The artist was accustomed to working up his landscapes with brown and blue washes, but in this instance he draws in the detail with the brush rather than the pen, producing a work of unusual freedom and beauty, which stands apart in his *oeuvre* when compared to such characteristic works with similar compositions as the two preliminary studies for the painting of *The Hilly Road* of 1603.[1]

Although his style was based on the landscapes of the brothers Mathijs and Paul Brill and Gillis van Conixloo, Brueghel had, by the time he made this drawing, developed an entirely personal manner, notable for its lightness of touch and delicacy in the use of coloured wash, seen particularly in the depiction of trees and fields in the left hand middleground of the present study. The drawing, probably done in the latter part of his career, has the appearance of a study based on actual landscape, possibly the rolling countryside to the south of Brussels towards the Ardennes. He was much celebrated as a landscape artist in his own lifetime.

---

[1] Dresden, the Albertina, Vienna and Kunsthistorisches Museum, Vienna respectively; Winner (1961), pp. 208-9, figs. 16–18.

Jan Harmensz. Muller

(b. Amsterdam 1571; d. Amsterdam 1628)

55　Moses and the Brazen Serpent

Pen and dark brown ink, grey wash, and white body-colour (oxidized), on paper washed with red chalk. 236 × 375.

Inscribed:

An° 1590; Spranger.

Collections:

William Young Ottley; Francis Douce, by whom bequeathed in 1834.

Selected literature:

Parker, I, no. 34 (as Cornelis van Haarlem); Hand, no. 88.

The subject, taken from the Book of Numbers (21. 4–9), illustrates God's punishment of the Israelites for expressing their discontent with life in the desert (see also no. 9). They were attacked by a plague of poisonous snakes, an event vividly represented by the numerous writhing bodies in contorted postures in the foreground. Instructed by God, Moses made a brass serpent which he mounted on a pole, which would cure all those victims who, having repented of their rebelliousness, looked upon the image. This principal scene, in which Moses is accompanied by Aaron standing beside the pole, is relegated to the background before an extensive mountainous landscape.

Ascribed by a former owner to Bartholomäus Spranger, and subsequently attributed to Cornelis van Haarlem, the drawing was only recently recognised as the work of Jan Muller, an Amsterdam artist who in the late 1580s had engraved the works of Cornelis van Haarlem and Hendrick Goltzius. The present drawing shows his successful absorption of the current Late Mannerist style in which they were still working, especially noticeable in the strongly foreshortened figures which are a feature of Cornelis van Haarlem's work; the latter also provided the source for individual figures in this drawing. The same nervous, angular penwork is found in another drawing by Muller dated 1590, which served as the preparatory study for his engraving of the *Baptism of Christ*.[1] Through his work as an engraver of the works of Spranger and Adriaen de Vries as well as the Haarlem artists, Muller became one of the principal disseminators of Late Mannerism throughout Europe.

---

[1] Munich; Hand, p. 230, fig. 1.

David Vinckboons

(b. Malines 1576; d. Amsterdam 1630/33)

56   A Rustic Feast

Pen and brown ink with grey wash. 260 × 343.

Inscribed:
>   *David...ppe.*

Collections:
>   Johann Goll van Franckenstein (L. 2987); Francis Douce, by whom bequeathed in 1834.

Selected literature:
>   Parker, I, no. 90; Goossens, p. 69, pl. 33; Lloyd (1982), no. 37.

The present drawing, which was probably intended as a preparatory study, was engraved in reverse by Pieter van Serwouters in 1608 with the title *Soo gewonnen-Soo geronnen* [Easy come, easy go] and the words *Swetsende bedelars* [Bragging beggars] inscribed above the inn sign. Unusually finished in execution, it represents the type of peasant scene covering a wide range of rustic behaviour which Vinckboons derived from his study of Pieter Bruegel the Elder. Although he emigrated from Flanders to Holland, he retained his native style, which he was influential in introducing into the Northern Netherlands. The composition of the present drawing relates generally to a painting of a *Peasant Dance*.[1] (Another painting, probably a copy, was made from the drawing.[2])

---

[1] Private collection, Warmond; Goossens, pl. 32.
[2] Private collection, Scheveningen; photograph in Museum files.

Peter Paul Rubens

(b. Siegen 1577; d. Antwerp 1640)

57 A nude Man seen partly from behind

Oiled charcoal, partly stumped and heightened with white chalk. 315 × 367.

Collections:
P. H. Lankrink (L. 2090); Chambers Hall (L. 551), by whom presented in 1855.

Selected literature:
Parker, I, no. 200; Burchard & d'Hulst, no. 57; Lloyd (1982), no. 38; Cleaver, no. 3.

Following the example of the Carracci and other contemporary Italian artists whose work he had studied in Italy, Rubens developed the practice of making large scale chalk studies from the model, usually after the composition of the final painting had been established in an oil-sketch. Such studies served both the master himself and any assistant involved in the execution of the final work.

The figure which appears here occurs first as one of the executioners in the *Raising of the Cross* (now in Grasse), which was painted for one of the side altars in S. Croce in Gerusalemme, Rome, in 1602, and subsequently as one of the figures supporting Christ in the *Raising of the Cross* (now in Antwerp Cathedral), painted for the high altar of St Walburga, Antwerp in 1610–11. As was usual with Rubens, the same pose also recurs in a number of later works. There has been much debate as for which composition this study was originally made, but given the scale of the sheet and the existence of a number of other similar studies made indisputably for the *Raising of the Cross*, it seems reasonable to associate it with that work, although the young model in the drawing was transformed into a much older bald man in the painting. The display of strength required for lifting a man is magnificently realised in this study.

Rubens was much concerned with the proportions of the human body, and in his unpublished treatise, while lamenting 'so many paunch-bellies, weak and pitiful arms and legs' seen today, he praised the kind of classical body perfected by strenuous training, particularly seen 'from the backs of porters, the arms of prize fighters, the legs of dancers, and almost the whole body of watermen'. The antique marble group of *Two Wrestlers* (Uffizi, Florence) as well as works by Tintoretto have been suggested as the source for the pose in this drawing.

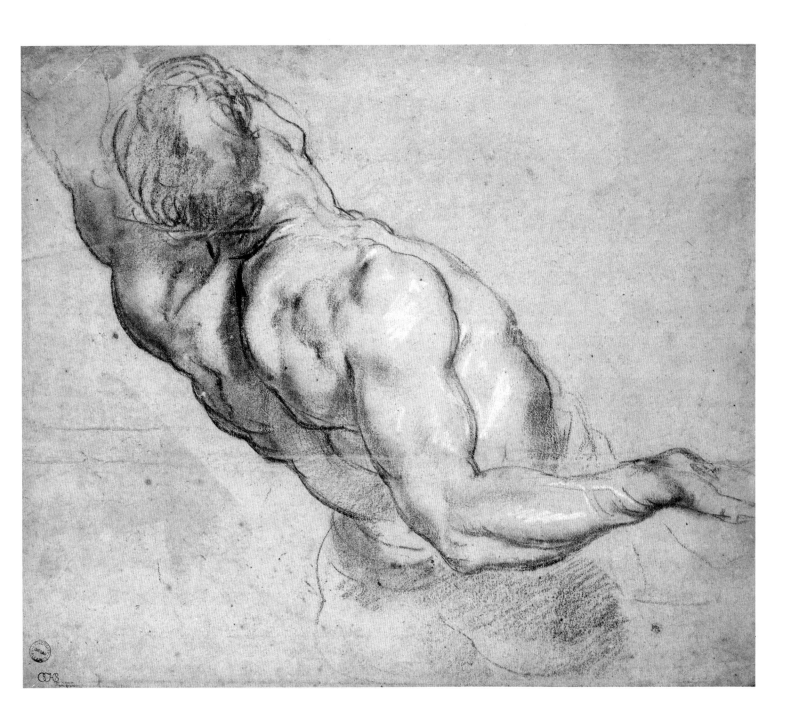

58 A female Nude reclining

Red chalk, heightened with touches of white.
250 × 178.

Inscribed:
    P P Rubens.

Collections:
    J. H. Hall. Purchased in 1954.

Selected literature:
    Cleaver, no. 4.

Despite the prevalence of the female nude in Rubens's paintings, there are, unlike in the case of Rembrandt, remarkably few examples among his drawings. Although it is recorded that Helena Fourment destroyed a number of paintings containing the female nude, it seems less likely that she would have done the same to his working drawings, since, according to the terms of the artist's will, these were to be kept together in case any of his children might become an artist. Rubens may very well have followed Renaissance practice, seen notably in the work of Michelangelo and Raphael, of using a male model for a female figure. (One such drawing by Rubens showing Psyche has the appearance of such an origin[1]). If made from the nude model, this drawing is, therefore, a rarity in the existing *oeuvre*.

There is another red chalk drawing, representing the same figure but seen from a different angle, which must have been made about the same time (fig. 2).[2] Unusually for Rubens, neither study can be connected with a known painting. On stylistic grounds they were probably drawn during the middle of the second decade, perhaps *c.* 1616.

It has been debated whether the two drawings represent the figure in the same pose studied from different viewpoints, or in two slightly different poses. In support of the latter contention, which would prove that the studies were made from the live model, it has been said that in the drawing formerly in Basel, the figure, who in both drawings is supporting her left arm on a cushion, leans further forward than she does in the Oxford drawing. But if the pose is the same in both drawings, it can equally well be argued that they were copied from a now lost small bronze or wax figure. The character of the drawing, with its fully realised modelling, is similar to other copies Rubens made after sculpture, and the type of figure with elongated neck is redolent of sixteenth century sculpture. But the different viewpoints make it very difficult to determine whether the pose is identical in both studies.

Fig. 2. Peter Paul Rubens, *Nude*

[1] Royal Collection, Windsor; Van Puyvelde, no. 279.
[2] Formerly in the Robert von Hirsch collection, Basel, sold Sotheby's, London, 20 June 1978, no. 34.

59 A woodland Scene

Black chalk with a few touches of red chalk and white body-colour. 383 × 499.

Collections:

P. H. Lankrink (L. 2090); Chambers Hall (L. 551), by whom presented in 1855.

Selected literature:

Parker, I, no. 201; Burchard & d'Hulst, no. 207; Adler, no. 74; Held, no. 228; Cleaver, no. 10.

Although Rubens made landscape paintings and drawings occasionally throughout his working life, it was only after his purchase of the Château de Steen in 1635 that he devoted a considerable amount of time to the practice. In his last years he spent an increasing amount of time in the country, as a result of which his landscape paintings form a substantial part of his *oeuvre* produced during these years.

The present drawing, which depicts a wooden bridge over a small river bordered by willows with a road lined with poplars, must have been executed about this time. Without any identifying features which could pinpoint the locality, the general character of the landscape is similar to that found around the Château de Steen. Although it is clear from their inscriptions that a number of landscape drawings were, unlike the paintings, made before the motif, the size and character of this drawing, with its carefully worked out composition, suggest that it was more likely to have been made in the studio. It shows the same lightness of touch, combined with masterly rendering of space, found in other late works such as the drawing of the *Landscape with a Wattle Fence* in the British Museum, London.[1]

The drawing does not relate closely to any known painting, although the wooden bridge is reminiscent of a similar bridge on the left hand side of the *Château de Steen,* in the National Gallery, London, and the group of willows and poplars are similar to those in the lost painting of *Horsemen at a Watering Place*, known from an engraving by Schelt a Bolswert.[2]

[1] Adler, no. 75.
[2] Adler, no. 60.

Cornelis Hendriksz. Vroom

(b. Haarlem *c.* 1591; d. Haarlem 1661)

60 A rocky Pinnacle dominating an Estuary, near Rives

Pen and brown ink. 162 × 229.

Inscribed:
>*Vroom..*

Inscribed on the *verso:*
>*bij rives; van de oude vroom.*

Collections:
>Lord Trewoen; Jowett; Baron Hatvany.
>Purchased in 1946.

Selected literature:
>Keyes, no. D29.

The drawing belongs to a group of landscape studies done along the river Rhône, some of which are identified views of, for example, Lyon, Vienne-sur-Rhône and Pont Esprit-sur-Rhône.[1] According to the inscription on the back, which may have been added by the artist, the location of the present sheet is identified as being near Rives. As has been noted neither Rive-de-Gier, between Lyon and Saint Etienne, nor Rives near Grenoble offers scenery similar to that in the drawing, although rocky cliffs are found along the river Isère not far from the latter.

Among the group of Rhône landscapes the present drawing, with its strong reminiscence of Pieter Bruegel the Elder's Alpine landscapes, is the most old-fashioned. (The jutting-out rock is a feature found in the older artist's work.) The signature or contemporary inscription which appears on a number of the sheets, including the present one, has in the past been taken to refer to Hendrick Vroom (an ascription supported here by a later annotator), who according to Van Mander was active in Lyon. But recently it has been argued that this visit must have taken place before 1590, when the elder Vroom became involved in designing tapestries in Delft, and such an early date is inconceivable for the style of the drawings. It has been proposed that they are by his son, Cornelis Vroom, whose early work closely follows that of his father. The authorship remains, however, uncertain. Although retaining the compositional formulae of the sixteenth century, these drawings display some of the naturalistic observation of the new realistic style of landscape introduced in Haarlem at the beginning of the seventeenth century.

---

[1] For a listing and discussion of the group, see Keyes, nos. D2, D9–11, D25 and D28.

Rembrandt Harmensz. van Rijn

(b. Leyden 1606; d. Amsterdam 1669)

61   Jael killing Sisera

Pen and brown ink. 174 × 255.

Collections:
> Viscount Fitzharris. Purchased in 1950.

Selected literature:
> Benesch, no. 622a; Lloyd (1982), no. 46.

The subject is taken from the Book of Judges (4. 17–21) and describes how Sisera, the leader of the defeated Canaanite army, is offered refuge by a woman called Jael in her tent or hut. Having fed him and put him to bed, she takes a hammer and drives a tent peg through his temple. Unlike the biblical account in which he dies immediately, Sisera in Rembrandt's drawing is shown furiously resisting the onslaught, kicking over in his agony a table at the end of the bed. In his attempt to extract the maximum drama and action, Rembrandt has redrawn the arms and legs so that it is now difficult to read exactly which limb belongs to whom. The artist started with relatively thin lines done with the quill pen, developing his study of violence and pain with the broad brush-like lines produced by the reed pen, which increasingly became his favourite tool for drawing. The melodrama of Sisera's murder is conveyed as much by the manner of execution as by the conception of the subject. An arched window can be seen on the left, but the roughly drawn shape on the right is difficult to read – it may be a curtain.

This drawing was probably executed about 1648–49. By this time Rembrandt in his illustrations of biblical themes was tending to concentrate on subjects limited to two protagonists, whose contrasting internal reactions to the event described was movingly conveyed by facial expression and gesture. As befits the violent nature of the subject, the present study is highly dramatic, unusually so for the period in which it was executed. When he illustrated the subject about ten years later in a drawing,[1] his interpretation was more contemplative and statically monumental. And characteristic of his practice when returning to a subject, by depicting Jael about to strike the first blow, he illustrates a slightly different moment in the story.

---

[1] Amsterdam; Benesch, no. 1042.

146

Rembrandt

62 Landscape with Farm Buildings beside a Road

Pen and ink and brown wash, heightened with white, with later additions in grey wash.
113 × 247.

Collections:
    Earl Spencer (L. 1531); Chambers Hall (L. 551), by whom presented in 1855.

Selected literature:
    Parker, I, no. 186; Benesch, no. 1227; Lloyd (1982), no. 47, Schneider, no. 22.

This drawing represents one of Rembrandt's favourite motifs, a farm surrounded by trees, here seen sited beside a road with the river bank rising up on the left. The daily life of the farm is revealed by the artist's attention to detail. The top of a covered haystack appears behind the chimney of the farm building, while a smaller stack can be seen between the gate on the left and the front door. At the rear of the building, a latch to trap doves extends from the roof; below at the side manure is piled up. In order to encompass the whole subject, Rembrandt had to add a piece of paper to the right hand side of his original sheet. As was his habit he used white body-colour to carry out refinements, here to remove the horizontal line on the grass on the right. The grey wash may have been added, as happened to other drawings, by a later hand. A copy reveals that the original drawing has been cut a little at the bottom, which slightly spoils the spatial effect.

The same farm building, but seen in reverse and with different surroundings, recurs in the etching of the *Landscape with a Fisherman*,[1] and the drawing may well have served for the central part of the latter. Both works were probably executed *c.* 1650–51 at the beginning of Rembrandt's last intensive period devoted to landscape prints and drawings. The central motif was probably studied on one of the artist's sketching tours in the vicinity of Amsterdam, and the recurrence of the same farm in other drawings may suggest that he was accompanied, as he was on other occasions, by a pupil or pupils.

This drawing is one of the most compact and magisterial landscapes, achieving through its closely worked penwork a harmony in rendering the basic features of the landscape bathed in light and atmosphere. The measured rendering of space, starting from the posts beside the diagonally receding road in the central foreground, establishes the central motif halfway back in the composition, with distant vistas opening up on either side.

---

[1] Hollstein, XVIII, pp. 103–04, no. B213.

Anthonie Waterloo

(b. Lille 1609/10; d. Utrecht 1690)

63 View of Rhenen

Black chalk heightened with white, with grey wash. 211 × 417.

Collections:
>   purchased in 1951.

The town of Rhenen, distinguishable by its Gothic church with a tall spire, is situated on the Rhine in the east of Holland. During the seventeenth century, it was studied by a large number of artists, of whom the most notable were Hercules Seghers and Jan van Goyen. It was conveniently located on the river on the way to Arnhem and Cleves, which served as the final destinations for a sketching tour much favoured by artists from the west of Holland at the time.

Waterloo was probably a self-taught artist, who also made a living as an art dealer. He was a prolific and attractive landscape draughtsman whose manner resembles that of Simon de Vlieger and Roelant Roghman. He usually worked in chalk and grey wash, often as here on blue or on other occasions on off-white paper. His subjects were predominantly woods or scenes in which the rays of the sun breaking through trees played a major part and, as here, panoramic views. Although a rare and rather stiff painter, he made a considerable number of etchings of similar subjects, including a *View of Rhenen*,[1] which convey the same qualities seen in his drawings. Apart from his views and studies made on sketching tours in Holland, he undertook an extensive tour through Germany going as far as Danzig (Gdansk).

[1] Wessely, no. 90.

150

Philips de Koninck

(b. Amsterdam 1619; d. Amsterdam 1688)

64 Half-length Figure of a Man

Black chalk. 140 × 100.

Inscribed:
P. Koning. f..
Inscribed on the *verso*:
P. Ko (in pen and ink) and: *1662* (in red chalk).

Collections:
Joseph van Haecken (L. 2516); J. H. Hall. Purchased in 1954.

Selected literature:
Sumowski, Drawings, VI, no. 1341.

What appears to be a genuine signature and the date occur on the back of the drawing; the inscription *P. Koning f.*, which appears on the front of the sheet, is the same as that found on other drawings by the artist and has been tentatively accepted as genuine. If the date of 1662 is correct, the drawing is a relatively late work, although it recalls Rembrandt's drawing style of the 1640s. Koninck had got to know Rembrandt after his move to Amsterdam in 1640, and, apart from apparently accompanying him on sketching tours along the River Amstel, was much influenced by the older artist's figure studies.

The study appears to have been made from the life. Koninck almost invariably drew in pen and ink and his use of chalk is most unusual. A similar although older figure wearing a bandanna occurs in the painting of *The Feast of Bacchus* of 1654.[1] The present model has the appearance of some of the eastern European refugees found in Amsterdam at the time, who were also studied by Rembrandt.

---

[1] Bredius Museum, The Hague; Sumowski, *Gemälde,* III, no. 1018.

Aelbert Cuyp

(b. Dordrecht 1620; d. Dordrecht 1691)

65   Landscape

Black chalk and black lead with grey and ochre washes. 108 × 218.

Collections:
    Charles Emmanuel, by whom presented in 1950.

The subject of this drawing is a characteristic valley landscape of the kind Cuyp made on his travels along the banks of the Rhine and the Meuse and in the vicinity of Cleves. In addition to the difficulty of identifying the locations of his motifs, hardly any of his drawings can be securely dated, but this appears to be an example of his mature style. Executed in coloured washes over black chalk in the foreground and black lead in the background, a combination which serves to increase the sense of distance and was first used by Cuyp, this landscape offers a fully realised representation of light and atmosphere equivalent to what he achieved in his golden-toned paintings. Few of his drawings relate directly to his paintings and, apart from recording his general experience of landscape, which informed his subsequent work on canvas, they were probably done as works in their own right.

Albrecht Dürer

(b. Nuremberg 1471; d. Nuremberg 1528)

66 Youth kneeling before a Potentate

Pen and black ink. 252 × 189.

Inscribed with monogram and *Robt Sutton 1754*.

Collections:
  Sir Robert Sutton; Dr E. H. Craddock. Purchased in 1954.

Selected literature:
  Winkler, no. 42; Parker, I, no. 283; Panofsky, no. 1249; Lloyd (1982), no. 2.

Watched by two men looking through a window, a young man is kneeling in a stone-vaulted chamber before an elderly potentate in a turban who bears a sceptre.

The drawing was probably made by Dürer following his apprenticeship, when he travelled widely in the north of Europe, possibly during his residence in Basel between 1492 and 1494. It shows the engraver's manner of drawing with elaborate cross-hatching which the young Dürer had learnt principally from his study of the graphic works of Martin Schongauer. It does not connect with any other known work of the artist, although the onlookers are reminiscent of the figures in the artist's early woodcut illustrations, *Ritter vom Turn* and *Das Narrenschiff*, and the view of buildings through the window recalls that in the woodcut of *St Jerome* of 1492.[1] On the basis of Dürer's *Self-Portrait* drawing of 1493,[2] the young man may be regarded as a portrait of the artist. Both his pose and his appearance foreshadow the figure of the Prodigal Son in the slightly later engraving of that subject, around 1496.[3]

The subject has never been satisfactorily explained and numerous alternatives have been proposed: Jacob departing from Isaac, Joseph and Pharoah, David before Saul, the return of the Prodigal Son, St John the Evangelist before Domitian and a posthumous miracle of St James the Greater, as well as an unidentified scene with a presentation made to a donor. It has also been suggested that the figures were drawn separately and that the artist had no subject in mind. It may be that the drawing was made as an illustration, but, in view of the style, it is more likely to have been destined for an engraving rather than a woodcut.

[1] Hollstein, VII, p. 183, no. 227.
[2] Metropolitan Museum, New York (Lehmann Collection); Winkler, no. 27.
[3] Hollstein, VII, p. 24, no. 28.

67   The Pleasures of the World

Pen and black ink. 211 × 330.

Collections:
  Francis Douce, by whom bequeathed in 1834.

Selected literature:
  Winkler, no. 163; Parker, I, no. 285; Panofsky, no. 874.

The subject of this drawing, executed either just before Dürer's first visit to Venice in 1495 or more probably shortly afterwards, remains unexplained. In essence it derives from the Love Garden scenes of earlier fifteenth-century German prints, but the mood is more extrovert, as witnessed by the behaviour of the two women dragging off a reluctant and struggling man on the left. In the centre, lovers are seated around a table; on the right, figures freely disport themselves in a bath-house open to the air, while in the background a knightly joust takes place watched by spectators before a large castle. Three men are busy dragging a fishing-net from the river in the upper left. The setting is a courtly Garden of Eden, where everyone is concentrating on pleasurable activities. But the key to the subject can be found in the lower right hand corner, where a girl is escorted by an old man, followed by the figure of Death. Clearly the artist intended some moralistic allegory. Lucas van Leyden's large engraving of the *Dance of the Magdalen*[1] of 1519 echoes this drawing, particularly in the figures of the old man and the girl. Dürer's uncertainty about the final arrangement of the subject is emphasised by the numerous *pentimenti*, such as the large tree trunk, lightly drawn in later on the right, as well as by the fact that he drew the subject on two different occasions, using different pens and different coloured inks. Compared with the more tightly controlled penwork in the *Youth kneeling before a Potentate* (no. 66), this sheet reveals a marvellous freedom in the handling of the pen. For the first time, Dürer combined a large number of small incidents within one composition. Though there is much in common with the drawings he made before he went to Venice, this drawing has a unity which stems from his study of Italian art.

[1] Bartsch, VII, pp. 402–03, no. 122.

Hans Burgkmair

(b. Augsburg 1473; d. Augsburg 1531)

68   Portrait of a young Man

Black chalk on discoloured white paper, the background washed over with light brown watercolour. 288 × 209.

Collections:
 Sir Joshua Reynolds (L. 2364); Francis Douce, by whom bequeathed in 1834.

Selected literature:
 Parker, I, no. 281; Lloyd (1982), no. 5.

There is some facial resemblance between the subject of this study and a painted portrait of uncertain authorship of Martin Schongauer,[1] dated 1483 (or possibly 1453), although the sitter in the latter wears a large flat cap and is differently dressed. If this painting is, as has been suggested,[2] by Burgkmair's father, Thoman, it might be supposed that the drawing is a free interpretation by Hans, who having worked with his father was apprenticed to Schongauer in Colmar from 1488 to 1490. There are several other portrait studies drawn by Burgkmair in the same free manner, two of which are dated 1519 and 1520.[3]

Apart from Hans Holbein the Elder, Burgkmair was the most important artist in Augsburg, where he was active as a painter, etcher and a designer of woodcuts, playing a decisive role in the development of the chiaroscuro woodcut.

---

[1] Munich; Buchner, no. 56.
[2] Baum, pp. 10–12 and Bernhard, pp. 17–18.
[3] Berlin, Dresden and British Museum, London.

Mathis Nithart Gothart, called Grünewald

(b. Würzburg *c.* 1480; d. Halle 1528)

69 An elderly Woman with clasped Hands

Black chalk. 377 × 236.

Signed:

[M]*athis.*

Inscribed:

Matsis; 2; Disses hatt Mathis von Ossenburg des Churfürst en v[on] Mentz Moler gemacht und wo der Mathis ge schriben findest das ha[tt] Er mit Eigener handt gemacht.

Collections:

Francis Douce, by whom bequeathed in 1834.

Selected literature:

Parker, I, no. 297; Ruhmer, no. XVI; Testori & Bianconi, no. 52; Baumgart, no. XII; Lloyd (1982), no. 7; Rowlands, no. 119.

Not only one of the most beautiful studies made by the artist, this is the only existing drawing which can claim to bear a genuine signature (seen above the woman's right shoulder). That this was inscribed by the artist, and not by another hand as is sometimes said, is specifically stated in the long inscription on the right of the sheet, which also establishes the correct name of the painter. It appears to have been written by Philipp Uffenbach, who, according to Joachim von Sandrart, owned an album of drawings by Grünewald. (Uffenbach was a pupil of Hans Grimmer, who in turn was a pupil of Grünewald, which probably explains Uffenbach's ownership of the album.)

Both the type of figure and the nervous, emotive use of black chalk are entirely characteristic of the small body of drawings by this artist, for the most part executed in soft black chalk, which rank in their power of expression with the finest drawings of Dürer, a quality which in Grünewald's case was carried over into his painting. The play of light over the face and body is unusually subtle and varied. Although executed as a study for either the Virgin or the Magdalen in one of the scenes of Christ's Passion, such as the *Crucifixion*, the *Lamentation* or the *Mater Dolorosa*, the drawing does not connect with any known work. (There is some affinity with the figure of the Magdalen in the large seventeenth century copy after a lost *Crucifixion*[1] by Grünewald.) The drawing can, however, be associated both in theme and style with another half-length study of a *Woman Mourning*.[2] Grünewald's drawings are very difficult to date but it is generally assumed that this sheet was drawn shortly before he started on the major work of his career, the *Isenheim Altar-piece*, painted *c.* 1512–15.

[1] Donaueshingen; Hagen, p. 250.
[2] Oskar Reinhart Collection, Winterthur; Ruhmer, no. XV.

162

Albrecht Altdorfer

(b. c. 1482/85; d. Regensburg 1538)

70   St Nicholas of Bari rebuking the Tempest

Pen and dark ink, heightened with wash in body-colour on brick-red prepared paper. 192 × 147.

Signed with monogram, and dated:
1508.

Collections:
Francis Douce, by whom bequeathed in 1834.

Selected literature:
Parker, I, no. 268; Winzinger, no. 5; Lloyd (1982), no. 8; Guillaud (1984), no. 5; Mielke, no. 21.

Taken from *The Golden Legend* of Jacopo da Voragine, the subject of the present drawing shows a 'posthumous' miracle of St Nicholas of Bari, when he appeared in answer to prayer and calmed the storm. He is represented here, hand raised in benediction, on the left, while a demon is shown clinging to the crow's nest at the top of the mast blown over by the wind.

Executed during Altdorfer's early maturity, this drawing is of particularly high quality. Compared with the drawings of a year or two earlier, with their stiffly posed figures, the present sheet, as well as another drawing of 1508, *A Wildman carrying an uprooted Tree*,[1] are executed with a vigour and freedom on prepared paper richly coloured with reddish-brown body-colour. The expressive style of the penwork vividly conveys the effects of the storm, contrasted with the miraculous apparition of the saint above the stern of the ship.

---

[1] British Museum, London; Rowlands, no. 127.

Nicolas Manuel Deutsch

(b. Bern 1484; d. Bern 1530)

71   Christ and the Woman taken in Adultery

Pen and brown ink with grey wash. 342 × 309.

Signed with monogram and dated:
1527.
Inscribed in a tablet:
Wer under üch an [ohne] sund ist, der Werff den Ersten Stein vff sy Johani ann viij Cap.

Collections:
Francis Douce, by whom bequeathed in 1834.

Selected literature:
Parker, I, no. 330; Wagner, no. 292; Lloyd (1982), no. 9; Rowlands, no. 181.

The subject is based on John 8. 1–11. The inscribed quotation ['He that is without sin among you, let him cast a stone at her'] is taken from Luther's German translation of the Bible published in 1522. The drawing, a late work by the artist, was made as a design for a glass-painting executed by an anonymous Bernese artist.[1] The drawing shows the artist's usual broad manner of execution and strong characterization of individual figures, while the lack of depth and the concentration on detail is typical of his late work. The same style is apparent in another stained glass design of the same year, *King Josiah destroying the Idols*.[2] The same composition recurs in the artist's *Dance of Death* (destroyed but recorded in copies), which he executed earlier, between 1516 and 1520.[3] But it seems likely that the scene of *Christ and the Woman taken in Adultery* was only added to this work, using the present drawing, in a subsequent repainting.

Together with the *Expulsion of the Money Changers from the Temple*, the present subject, seen again in other works by Lucas Cranach and his school, was popular among reformers as an allegory of the current ecclesiastical corruption and hypocrisy. In addition to being an artist and poet, Manuel Deutsch was active as a politician and diplomat, and his last years were devoted to promoting the Reformation. It is possible that a wall painting of the subject may have been considered by Hans Holbein the Younger for his decoration of the Council Chamber in the town hall at Basel, the final phase of which was carried out shortly after this drawing.

[1] Bad Schinznach; Wagner, pl. 169. The glass-painting is inscribed below the composition, presumably at a later date, with the arms of Samuel Jener and the date 1697. For the various copies of the Ashmolean drawing, see Rowlands, no. 181.
[2] Basel; Wagner, no. 295.
[3] Formerly in the Dominican Priory, Bern; see Rowlands, under no. 181.

Urs Graf

(b. Solothurn *c.* 1485; d. ?Basel 1529/30)

72 A mercenary Soldier and a Monster

Pen and black ink. 207 × 155.

Inscribed:
1518.

Collections:
Francis Douce, by whom bequeathed in 1834.

Selected literature:
Parker, I, no. 296; Lloyd (1982), no. 11; Rowlands, no. 184.

Based on his experiences as a mercenary in various expeditions in Italy and Burgundy between 1510 and 1522, Graf made a number of drawings of soldiers, often satirical in intent. Here a mercenary is portrayed with a fantastic creature on the banks of a lake bordered by mountains. A similar monster had already appeared in a drawing of 1512 in company with a monk and again in a drawing of 1516 with a mercenary soldier.[1] The present sheet has been cut at the bottom and possibly, in view of the unusual absence of the artist's monogram, at the sides as well. It is a characteristic example of Graf's vivid and calligraphic handling of the pen in his drawings, which, unusually for contemporary German art, were often done, as appears to be the case here, as works in their own right.

Although the soldier is not identified with the usual signs, such as a cross of St Andrew on his cloak, it is clear that, with his long drooping beard and down-at-heel appearance, he is intended to represent one of the German mercenaries who were much hated as rivals by their Swiss counterparts, and much feared as agents of plunder and assault by the citizenry. The artist himself was no stranger to the violent life of a mercenary and was guilty on a number of occasions of assault, beating his wife and a variety of other offences.

---

[1] Both in Basel; Koegler, nos. 17 and 20.

Sebald Beham

(b. Nuremberg 1500; d. Frankfurt-am-Main 1550)

73　The Temptation of Christ

Pen and brown ink, with grey and pink watercolours. 227 in diameter.

Collections:
　　Francis Douce, by whom presented in 1834.

Selected literature:
　　Parker, I, no. 275.

This drawing, the subject of which is taken from Luke 4. 1–13, belongs to a series of at least twenty-five scenes from the life of Christ, carried out by Beham as designs for roundels of stained glass. With the *Multiplication of the Bread and Fishes*[1] and the *Massacre of the Innocents*,[2] the present study forms a group within the series, notable for the use of coloured washes and a more finished technique. The *Massacre of the Innocents* and one other drawing are dated 1522, establishing that they were executed before he was banished from Nuremberg in 1525 for his open espousal of the Peasants' War. His early works, which include the present series of roundels, show the strong influence of Dürer's art, of, for example, the *Last Supper*[3] of 1523, the only woodcut executed from what appears from a group of ten drawings to have been intended as a Passion series in a large oblong format. (An ascription to Dürer occurs on many drawings from the present series by Beham.)

---

[1] Oxford; Parker, I, no. 274.
[2] Berlin.
[3] Hollstein, VII, p. 149, no. 184.

Daniel Lindtmayer the Younger

(b. Schaffhausen 1552; d. Lucerne 1606/07)

74 The Almighty creating the Sun and the Moon

Pen and black and brown inks. 264 × 190.

Signed with monogram and dated:
1571.

Collections:
H. R. Lando (L. 1658); A S (L. 173ᵃ).
Purchased in 1948.

Selected literature:
Falk, p. 123.

The drawing illustrates the beginning of the world as described in Genesis 1. 1–16: 'And God made two great lights; the greater light to rule the day, and the lesser light to rule the night'.

In 1605 the drawing belonged to Hans Rudolf Lando (1584–1646), who inscribed his signature and the date lower right. But despite the fact that Lando is recorded as a specialist collector of stained glass drawings and that Lindtmayer made numerous designs for the medium, the present drawing is unlikely to have been made for this purpose. The precise, hatched manner of execution suggests that it was more probably done with a print in mind. He made a number of engravings and woodcuts as well as book illustrations, including some of the woodcut illustrations to Stimmer's Bible, published at Basel in 1576. Signed with monogram and dated 1571, this is the earliest documented drawing known by Lindtmayer, who belonged to a family of artists in Schaffhausen.

Claude Gellée, called Claude Lorrain

(b. Chamagne 1600; d. Rome 1682)

75 A Farm House in the Campagna

Pen and brown ink and wash over black chalk.
122 × 184.

Inscribed:
   1663 ott..^{bre} 4 Claud.

Collections:
   Jonathan Richardson, Senior (L. 2183);
Chambers Hall (L. 551), by whom presented in
1855.

Selected literature:
   Parker, I, no. 400; Roethlisberger (1968),
no. 908.

Parker identified the subject of this drawing as the Torre de Quinto, at the northern end of the Ponte Molle on the Tiber. However, Roethlisberger has pointed out that the tower of that farm house was square, and that this building with a round tower was situated at the opposite end of the bridge, which can be seen in the distance on the right. It is one of many such farm houses which could be found all over the Campagna until the nineteenth century. A companion drawing in the Ashmolean, probably made at the same time, shows a different view of the same building.[1] Claude made numerous other views of the Ponte Molle, both paintings and drawings, particularly in the 1740s. Most show the bridge looking towards the square Torre de Quinto,[2] but the round tower is incorporated in several paintings of idyllic landscapes.[3] Both farm houses can be seen, to splendid effect, in a *Pastoral Landscape* of 1645.[4]

Finished nature studies are perhaps the least common of Claude's drawings. This sheet was made in the open air: the pen work is very rapid and scribbling, and the wash applied equally quickly to add light and shade to the landscape. It is likely that, although they provided elements for larger compositions, such informal works were made primarily for the artist's pleasure.

---

[1] Parker, I, no. 412; Roethlisberger (1968), no. 909.
[2] Roethlisberger (1968), nos. 145, 426, 427, 736, 859, 860, 908 and 909.
[3] Roethlisberger (1961), nos. LV 64, LV 83.
[4] City Museum and Art Gallery, Birmingham; Roethlisberger (1961), no. LV 90.

Claude

76 Landscape with Ascanius shooting the Stag of Silvia

Pen and brown ink and wash, touched with body-colour, with horizon and perspective lines in black chalk. 248 × 315.

Signed, dated and inscribed:
Claudio f. 1682; libro. 7. di. Vigilio; Come Ascanio saettà il ceruo. di. silvia. figliola. di. Tirro Roma 1681 Claudio I. U. F.

Collections:
Arthur Pond; John Barnard (L. 1420); Lord Palmerston; Lord Northbrook; Mrs W. F. R. Weldon, by whom presented in 1926.

Selected literature:
Parker, I, no. 402; Roethlisberger (1968), no. 1128; Kitson, no. 112; Lloyd (1982), no. 85.

Claude's last painting, *Landscape with Ascanius shooting the Stag of Silvia*,[1] was commissioned as one of a pair by the most assiduous patron of Claude's later years, Prince Lorenzo Onofria Colonna, Grand Constable of the Kingdom of Naples; its pendant, *View of Carthage with Dido, Æneas and their Suite leaving for the Hunt*, was completed some years earlier, in 1676.[2] The subject owes something to an earlier painting of 1672, showing *The Coast of Libya with Æneas hunting*, and its preparatory drawings of 1669.[3] As the inscriptions on both the painting and this drawing state, the subject is found in Book VII of Virgil's *Æneid*: after the Trojans have landed in Latium, Ascanius, the son of Æneas, goes out hunting with his followers. Incensed by the Fury Allecto, he shoots the tame stag adopted by Silvia, daughter of Tyrrhus, guardian of the herds of King Latinus. As a result, war breaks out between the Trojans and King Latinus, with the prize being the area later to become Rome.

Claude made only two preparatory drawings for the painting. The first, dated 1678,[4] shows the group of hunters in a clearing, with trees set back in the middle distance. There is no river, and no fortified hill town on top of crags on the right. In fact, the scene follows closely Virgil's description of an isolated and uninhabited countryside. By early 1682, the date of the Oxford drawing, Claude had introduced the ruined antique temple on the left, and removed the hillside on the right. In the background can be seen a bay on the coast, with ships, and hills on the horizon. The foliage is drawn with extraordinary delicacy, and the use of perspective lines allows the scene to fade into the distance. When Claude came to the painting, he made further changes, opening up the temple, inserting a fathomless river between the hunter and his prey, and allowing the atmosphere to dissolve into rolling blue plains. The figures are even more elongated and insubstantial, and the tonality confined to evanescent and powdery blue. The painting and its final preparatory study are both deeply moving, the intensely personal elegy of a very old man.

---

[1] Ashmolean Museum, Oxford, A376; Roethlisberger (1961), no. 222.
[2] Kunsthalle, Hamburg; Roethlisberger (1961), no. LV 186.
[3] Roethlisberger (1961), no. LV 180, and Roethlisberger (1968), nos. 990–92.
[4] Chatsworth; Roethlisberger (1968), no. 1127.

Charles Le Brun

(b. Paris 1619; d. Paris 1690)

77   The penitent Magdalen

Red chalk heightened with white. 330 × 268.

Inscribed:
> *Le Brun.*

Collections:
> Sir Thomas Lawrence (L. 2445). Purchased in 1956.

Le Brun's painting of the *Penitent Magdalen*[1] was commissioned by the Abbé Le Camus, probably in 1656–57, for the Carmelite Convent in the rue St Jacques, Paris. The decoration of their church was an important undertaking, for which Le Brun was largely responsible: he made four principal paintings, and several others for various subsidiary chapels. The *Magdalen* was placed as the altar-piece in the chapel dedicated to St Charles, along with six smaller paintings illustrating the life of Mary Magdalen, executed by Le Brun's pupils after drawings by the master. It became one of the artist's most celebrated works, and Gérard Edelinck's engraving after it was widely distributed. Contemporaries particularly admired the 'noble expression of the passions', conveyed in the facial expression, the disorder of the draperies, the awkward position of the body, and the chaos in the room itself.

This figure study represents one stage of the picture's development: the head was no doubt drawn separately, and benefits from Le Brun's examination of the Passions – his lectures on this subject were not given until 1668, but he had been interested in it long before this date. There is no truth in the view, widely believed until recently, that Louis XIV's favourite, Mlle de la Vallière, was the model for this figure.

---

[1] Musée du Louvre, Paris; Thuillier & Montagu, no. 25.

Antoine Watteau

(b. Valenciennes 1684; d. Nogent-sur-Marne 1721)

78 Girl seated with a Book of Music on her Lap

Black, white and red chalks on greyish paper.
245 × 156.

Collections:
   Miss James; Mrs Emma Joseph, by whom presented in 1942.

Selected literature:
   Parker & Mathey, no. 552; Lloyd (1982), no. 90.

As Watteau's biographer the comte de Caylus wrote, 'Ordinarily, he drew without any special aim. For he never made a sketch or a study for any of his paintings, however light and unfinished they were. His habit was to draw his studies in a bound volume, so that he always had a great many available . . . When he decided to paint a picture, he made use of this volume. He chose the figures best suited to his needs at that moment. He made up his groups with them, usually according to the landscape background he had prepared'.[1] Many of these figure studies were engraved for the *Figures de différents caractères*, a volume of plates after drawings by Watteau. Indeed, this drawing was engraved by Benoit Audran for inclusion in the collection, but inexplicably omitted from the final publication.[2]

It is therefore not surprising that this charming figure of a young girl following a musical score should be found, with slight adjustments, in at least two of Watteau's paintings, *Le Concert* and *Pour nous prouver que cette belle*, both of which have been dated *c.* 1716–18.[3] The drawing, in the technique Watteau developed of 'trois crayons', black, white and red chalks, is graceful and remarkably fluent. The effect of light shimmering on the grey silk of the skirt is particularly well caught, and this ability, evident too in many of his paintings, is one especially appreciated by Caylus.

[1] Caylus, p. 24.
[2] The print was inserted in the copy of the *Figures* belonging to the Bibliothèque de l'Arsenal, Paris: see Dacier & Vuaflart, I, p. 132.
[3] Schloss Charlottenburg, Berlin, and Wallace Collection, London; Camesasca nos. 179 and 154.

79   Studies of a Spaniel

Red chalk. 159 × 109.

Collections:
Sir Karl Parker, by whom presented in 1953.

Selected literature:
Parker & Mathey, no. 896.

Despite the presence of a large number of domestic animals in Watteau's paintings, relatively few drawings of them survive, and they do not feature in the *Figures de différents caractères*. During his period as a pupil of Claude III Audran, curator of the Palais du Luxembourg, Watteau would have had ample opportunity to study Rubens's cycle of *The Life of Marie de Medici*, and certainly the dogs in his paintings can be seen in part as homage to the great Flemish master. In addition, the toy spaniel was a necessary accessory for any fashionable lady, and this larger spaniel was also popular: he appears, sleeping contentedly, in the painting *L'Amour paisible* of *c*. 1716–18.[1] In this beautiful drawing, he is caught with his head resting on his paw, and brilliantly realised. Watteau also restudied in a few more strokes the head of the dog, from a slightly different angle, retaining the same peaceful sense of repose.

[1] Schloss Charlottenburg, Berlin; Camesasca, no. 174.

Jean Baptiste Oudry

(b. Paris 1686; d. Beauvais 1755)

80   Head of a Wolf

Black, white and red chalks on blue paper.
294 × 306.

Collections:
    purchased in 1952.

Selected literature:
    Parker (1952), p. 55; Garlick, no. 83.

As the celebrated connoisseur P.-J. Mariette noted, Oudry's animal drawings are immediately striking. It is perhaps surprising, therefore, that the artist retained almost all of them until his death, save a group ceded to his important patron Ludwig II, Duke of Mecklenburg-Schwerin. Many of these studies were made from the life, particularly from specimens in the Menagerie at Versailles. This *Head of a Wolf*, however, is related to the final painting in Oudry's series of nine *Chasses royales*, commissioned by Louis XV for his various residences between 1733 and 1746. The painting, *La Chasse au loup*,[1] was made for the dining room of the Château de la Muette, a hunting lodge in the Bois de Boulogne, and was exhibited at the Salon of 1746. It shows a 'loup monstrueux', which had strayed into the park at Versailles, being set upon by four of the King's best dogs. La Font de Saint Yenne expressed great admiration for the painting, and in particular the skill with which Oudry captured the expression of the animals' fury, and the realism of the depiction of the fur of each beast.[2] These qualities can also be seen in the drawing, which conveys, even more vividly, the terror and fury of the wolf at bay. The use of 'trois crayons' on blue paper makes it probable that this sheet, like similar animal studies, was made after the painting,[3] in the full maturity of Oudry's development as the greatest *animalier* of the eighteenth century.

---

[1] Musée International de la Chasse, Gien; Opperman (1977), no. P192.
[2] La Font de Saint Yenne, p. 68.
[3] See Opperman (1966), especially pp. 394–96.

François Boucher

(b. Paris 1703; d. Paris 1770)

81 Young Girl carrying a Dog

Black chalk. 175 × 125.

Collections:

B. A. Blondel d'Azincourt; R. H. Randall Davies; Francis Falconer Madan, by whom bequeathed in 1962.

Selected literature:

Garlick, no. 62; Jean-Richard, under no. 636.

Boucher made a large number of similar drawings of single figures, either in red chalk or in black. This example shows his characteristic economy of means, and the charm of his clothed figures. The young girl, whom Mme Jean-Richard describes as a 'jeune paysanne', though there is nothing of the peasant about her, is seen from the back, holding a dog under her right arm, its tail dangling. She is drawn quickly but firmly, her neck long and graceful, and her features indicated in two or three short strokes.

Such drawings were probably made specifically to be reproduced as engravings. Indeed, the first owner of this sheet, the financier Blondel d'Azincourt, was an amateur engraver in the chalk manner, and made several prints after Boucher drawings in his own collection.[1] This drawing was, however, engraved by Boucher's friend Gilles Demarteau, in sanguine, along with its companion, now lost, of a boy seen from behind carrying a basket of flowers.[2]

---

[1] Jean-Richard, nos. 305–310.
[2] Jean-Richard, no. 635.

Jean Baptiste Greuze

(b. Tournus 1725; d. Paris 1805)

82 Kneeling Woman holding a Child

Red chalk. 269 × 216.

Collections:
> purchased in 1953.

Selected literature:
> Lloyd (1982), no. 93.

From his childhood, Greuze was an indefatigable draughtsman, and this habit later became almost an obsession. He made innumerable studies for each of his paintings, often with only minute differences between each one. As Greuze's great champion Diderot wrote in his *Salon de 1763*, 'He makes endless studies; he spares neither time nor money to obtain suitable models . . . He is a tireless observer in the street, at church, at the market, at the theatre, in the promenades, at public meetings. When he is meditating on a subject, he becomes obsessed by it, followed by it everywhere'.[1] Studies done from life were generally in red chalk, as is the case here, while compositional experiments were executed in pen and ink.

As is to be expected from this exponent of 'la peinture morale', a large number of his paintings and drawings depict domestic scenes, often involving mothers and children. Greuze was particularly interested in the education of the young child, as can be seen in many paintings.[2] This drawing, clearly made from life, is not connected with any known painting. It shows a robust child supported by his mother on the edge of his cradle. The technique is more energetic than usual in such studies, indicating that it was drawn very quickly – the pose must in any case have been only momentary. The mother has about her an air of the antique, with statuesque features, a 'Roman' hair style, and flowing dress, perhaps suggesting that the sheet dates from Greuze's 'classical' phase in the 1760s.

[1] Diderot, p. 236.
[2] For example, Munhall, nos. 23, 41–43.

Jean-Honoré Fragonard

(b. Grasse 1732; d. Paris 1806)

83 The sad Situation of Don Quixote and Sancho Panza, ill-treated by the Galley Slaves

Black chalk and brown wash. 418 × 288.

Collections:

Baron Dominique Vivant-Denon; Albert Meyer; Henry Oppenheimer; Francis Falconer Madan, by whom bequeathed in 1962.

Selected literature:

Ananoff, under no. 2667 (as Alexandre-Évariste Fragonard); Garlick, no. 72; Rosenberg, pp. 508–09.

Vivant-Denon owned a group of nineteen drawings by Fragonard illustrating scenes from Don Quixote, and of these, he made etchings after eight, including the present drawing.[1] The etching clarifies the disagreement which has grown up about the particular episode illustrated: because Don Quixote was knocked over on several occasions, the scene depicted has been identified as that after the Battle of the Sheep, or the attack on the wind mills, or the attack of the Yanquesians. Vivant-Denon's print is entitled *Triste situation de Don Quichotte et Sancho, maltraités par les galériens*, and the drawing shows the results of Don Quixote's misguided attempts to free criminals condemned to serve in the King's galleys: having driven away their guards, the Don asks them to take their chains to Toboso to relate what has happened and plea his cause to Lady Dulcinea. This the prisoners decline to do, and instead turn on their liberator and his servant and pelt them with stones, before fleeing into the mountains. The unfortunate pair are left in a sorry state (Book III, chapter 8).

Cervantes's picaresque novel enjoyed great popularity in eighteenth century France, and the translation by Filleau de Saint-Martin was reprinted at least twenty times between 1730 and 1780. It inspired remarkable suites of paintings by Natoire, and by Charles Coypel, both of which served as tapestry designs.[2] Unlike these, Fragonard's illustrations show nothing of the theatricality of the Opéra Comique, but instead great wit and some pathos. The technique is comparable to that in Fragonard's drawings for Ariosto's *Orlando Furioso*, with thick black chalk boldly used, and brown wash applied with great bravura. Both series are difficult to date, but they were probably made in the 1780s, and the similarity of Don Quixote's armour to that of Rinaldo suggests that they may be closely contemporaneous.[3] These drawings were clearly not intended to be engraved; it is no fault of Vivant-Denon's that he was unable to capture their spirit. They may, however, have been designed to be inserted in a copy of the text, like Fragonard's second set of illustrations for La Fontaine's *Contes*, bound in a sumptuous manuscript volume, but it is unlikely that this was ever so with the *Don Quixote* drawings.

[1] *The Illustrated Bartsch,* vol. 121, part 1, pp. 272–75, nos. 12101.333–12101.340.
[2] Both series of paintings are in the Musée national du Château de Compiègne.
[3] The quality of the *Don Quixote* drawings, and their style, preclude any acceptance of Ananoff's reattribution of them to Fragonard's son, Alexandre-Évariste.

Hubert Robert

(b. Paris 1733; d. Paris 1808)

84   An Italian Villa

Red chalk. 293 in diameter.

Collections:
François Renaud (L. 1042). Presented by Sir Karl Parker in 1978.

Hubert Robert accompanied the comte de Stainville, later the duc de Choiseul, to Rome in 1754, and remained there until 1765. During this time, he made innumerable drawings in red chalk, of both real and imaginary sites.

This splendid example of Robert's vivacious and secure style shows an unknown location in the Campagna. From the presence of the aqueducts in the background on the left, it may be supposed that the rather dilapidated villa was to be found in the Aniene valley above Tivoli. The sheet is unusual in shape, and may be dated *c.* 1764–66 by comparison with other circular sheets.[1] The motif of the women washing in the fountain is one which recurs very often in Robert's work, as does the child sitting playing with the dog. The warm, sunlit atmosphere, crumbling masonry and varied landscape explain why Robert should have so favoured this type of scene. It was also popular with collectors, who had such drawings mounted by leading craftsmen like François Renaud, as is the case here.

---

[1] Cailleux, no. 46.

Jean-Baptiste Hüet

(b. Paris 1745; d. Paris 1811)

85   Studies of Gourds

Water- and body-colours. 253 × 384.

Signed:
>   *j. B. hüet. 1785..*, and inscribed *1*.

Collections:
>   Percy Moore Turner, by whom presented in 1942.

Selected literature:
>   Garlick, no. 78.

The two principal influences on Hüet's art were François Boucher, who taught Hüet's teacher Le Prince and who may have given Hüet himself informal lessons; and Jean-Baptiste Oudry. From these masters, Hüet developed his favourite subject matter, *pastorales* and animal studies, and his technique of painting in oils and drawing in chalk. More original are his many etchings, usually of animals, and his drawings of botanical specimens. Hüet's plant studies are not uncommon,[1] but finished water-colour drawings of fruits and vegetables are rare in his *oeuvre*. These gourds are depicted with astonishing virtuosity, the rough surface with sharp brush strokes, and the smoother areas with long calm strokes. The gradations in colour are exquisitely managed, and it is particularly remarkable that there seems to be no chalk under-drawing. These studies are related to a sheet of ears of corn, recently exhibited in London, which display the same consummate skill in the 'characterization' of texture.[2] The function of this series is not known; the other drawing is dated 1792, and numbered *14*, in different ink, suggesting that the sheets were gathered together some years after they were made. It is possible that they were intended for teaching purposes, like the collection of engravings after Hüet published in 1805. Alternatively, they may have been extraordinarily sophisticated models for an accomplished colour engraver. As works of art in their own right, they have nothing of the dryness of the contemporary botanical drawings of, for example, Anne Vallayer-Coster, and are unique in the art of the period.

[1] See the dismembered sketch book: Prouté (1986), nos. 32–35, and Prouté (1988), nos. 27–31.
[2] Rothschild, no. 38; now Pierpont Morgan Library, New York.

Jean-Auguste-Dominique Ingres

(b. Montauban 1780; d. Paris 1867)

86   Portrait of an unknown Man

Graphite. 80 in diameter.

Signed:
> *jngres.*

Collections:
> David David-Weill; Sir Charles Clore.
> Purchased in 1986.

Selected literature:
> Naef, IV, no. 14.

For Ingres, painting and drawing portraits was always lucrative, though in later life, he declared it a 'waste of time', a distraction unworthy of a history painter.[1] He was a precocious draughtsman, and this portrait miniature and its companion[2] are among the earliest of his drawings to survive. They were made in 1797, when Ingres was seventeen, shortly before he left Toulouse for Paris to begin his studies in David's studio. For reasons difficult to understand, these two miraculously fine drawings have been confused with the work of Ingres's father, Jean-Marie-Joseph, whose portraits betray a provincial naivety completely lacking in his son's sophisticated characterizations.[3]

Although the format of this miniature is traditional, popularised in a long series of profile heads by Cochin, many of them engraved, the technique is already highly individual, but much less linear than it was to become in the larger portrait drawings, particularly of tourists in Rome. The minute and intricate depiction of each surface, of hair, flesh, and the ribbed silk coat, attest to the artist's precocity. The identity of the sitter is unfortunately not known, although he is probably related to the man in the companion drawing. Nor has his uniform been conclusively identified: it has been described as that of a 'legislator', but is more likely to belong to an army officer.

---

[1] 'C'est une perte de temps considérable': letter of 27 February 1826 to his friend Gilibert; Boyer d'Agen, p. 132.
[2] Musée du Louvre, Paris; Naef, IV, no. 13.
[3] Works by Ingres *père* are reproduced in Lapauze, pp. 4–10. The astonishing persistence of this misattribution is chronicled in Naef, I, pp. 44–46.

Hans Holbein the Younger

(b. Augsburg 1497; d. London 1543)

87   A young Englishwoman

Tip of the brush with black ink and water-colours, the outline indented with the stylus. 160 × 92.

Inscribed in ink, by a later hand:
> H: Holbeen.

Collections:
> Francis Douce, by whom bequeathed in 1834.

Selected literature:
> Parker, I, no. 298; Ganz, no. 151; Brown (1982), no. 4; Brown (1983), no. 3.

Although engraved in the eighteenth century by Christian von Mechel with the title *A Young Woman of the City of Basil*, it is much more likely that the subject of this famous drawing was an English middle class woman. What is essentially a costume study is nicely combined with naturalistic observation of the female figure, seen in the way the woman is depicted lifting her skirt above her ankle. It was originally thought that the study was made during Holbein's first stay in England *c*. 1526–28, and that the subject was perhaps a member of Sir Thomas More's house-hold, but it is far more probable that it was executed at some time during the second English visit from 1532 to 1543. Another similar study of *Two views of the same Lady wearing an English Hood*,[1] concentrating on the costume and headdress, was probably made around the same period. Although usually described as drawn with the pen, it is more likely that it was executed with the tip of the brush, demonstrating the artist's mastery and control.

The drawing was known to Rembrandt, who made a fairly careful copy, although he gave the figure a fuller, more characteristically Dutch face.[2] If, as has been surmised, the Holbein drawing actually belonged to Rembrandt, it may have been kept in the album 'full of curious miniature drawings . . . of all kinds of costume' described in the 1656 inventory of his collection. Rembrandt appears to have adapted the motif to the figure of the servant girl on the right of the drawing of *Lot and his family leaving Sodom*[3] Sir Joshua Reynolds also apparently made an adaptation of the figure, without the veil and tassels, either from Holbein's original or from Von Mechel's print.[4]

---

[1] British Museum, London; Rowlands, no. 197.
[2] Oslo; Van Regteren Altena (1967), pp. 377–8.
[3] British Museum, London; Benesch, IV, no. A36.
[4] Herrmann, p. 657.

Peter Lely

(b. Soest 1618; d. London, 1680)

88   Studies of Hands

Black, red and white chalks on buff paper.
382 × 268.

Collections:
    Sir Peter Lely (L. 2092); Thomas Hudson (L. 2432, twice); Maurice Marignane (L. 1872). Purchased in 1937.

Selected literature:
    Millar (1978), no. 65; Lloyd, no. 55; Brown (1982), no. 156; Brown (1983), no. 8; Stainton and White, no. 92.

Lely, a Dutch artist who came to England in 1641 or 1643 and later became Charles II's Principal Painter, left behind, in addition to the large number of paintings, a considerable body of finished portrait drawings. He does not, however, appear to have made complete studies from the life for his painted portraits, confining himself, as in this sheet, to studies of individual details. At least three other similar sheets of studies are known.[1] His method of working is recorded by the amateur painter Charles Beale, who notes that when painting his son, Lely made a drawing 'after an Indian gown which he had put on his back, in order to the finishing of the drapery of it'.

These three studies are connected with two portraits which form part of the celebrated series of 'Windsor Beauties' painted for the Duke and Duchess of York in the 1660s. (In 1685 the Duke became King James II.) The study at the top, and that on the lower right of the hand shown holding a shepherd's crook(?), were made for the portrait of *Mary Bagot, Countess of Falmouth*, probably painted *c.* 1664–65; that on the lower left is for the portrait of *Frances Stuart, Duchess of Richmond*, one of the earliest in the series, painted not later than *c.* 1662.[2] (Her other hand is shown holding a bow.) The variation in the position of the hands was an important element in providing variety in a series which might easily have become monotonously repetitive. Such studies, among which these rank as some of the most sensitive in the delineation of the hands, could have served studio assistants, increasingly used by Lely to meet the pressure of commissions, but in the event this series of portraits appears to have been entirely executed by the master himself.

---

[1] Courtauld Institute of Art, London; Millar (1978), nos. 66–68.
[2] Both at Hampton Court; Millar (1963), nos. 259 and 258.

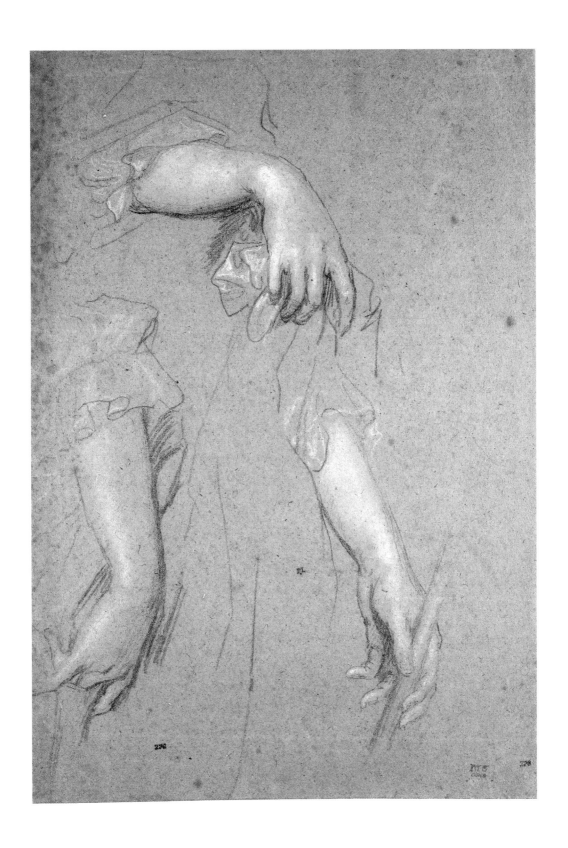

89 Sir Henry de Vic, Chancellor of the Order of the Garter

Black oiled chalk, heightened with white, on blue-grey paper. 490 × 318.

Inscribed in black chalk by a later hand: *Chancellor of the Order*.

Collections:

A. H. Sutherland; Mrs A. H. Sutherland, by whom presented to the Bodleian Library in 1837; placed on deposit in the Ashmolean Museum in 1950.

Selected literature:

Millar (1978), no. 114; Brown (1982), no. 154.

Sir Henry de Vic (*c.* 1599–1671), who had been English Resident at Brussels during the reign of Charles I, was later in exile with Charles II in the Netherlands. Following the Restoration of the Monarchy in 1660, the ceremonies connected with the Order of the Garter, the prime order of chivalry during the Stuart period, were revived with full splendour and the knights were given newly designed dress. De Vic was created Chancellor of the Order and in 1672 another member, Elias Ashmole, Windsor Herald and founder of the Ashmolean Museum, published an account of the Order.

The most outstanding group of drawings, not only in Lely's work but in Restoration England, are the thirty or more sheets known today representing the various knights who participated in the Procession of the Order of the Garter. All are full-length studies, sometimes confined to one figure, in other examples to two, executed on a grand scale and to a high degree of finish in black chalk heightened with white body-colour on blue-grey paper. Given the acuteness and variety of observation combined with the sense of movement, they must be the direct result of study of one of the annual processions; the richness of the dress, as the present example shows, is particulary fully realised in Lely's drawings. (By comparison Wenceslaus Hollar's etching of the procession is static and stereotyped.) From the knights represented, it can be deduced that the earliest date of the series is probably 1663 and the latest 1671, when the present sitter died.

But there is no record of any ultimate purpose for such a major task. About 1638, Van Dyck had painted an oil-sketch for Charles I, which later belonged to Lely, of the procession of the Order on St George's Day which remains the only record of a projected decoration of a room in Whitehall before the Civil War. It may be that in emulation of this, Lely was contemplating a similar grandiose scheme of decoration. Or the drawings may have been made as an end in themselves.[1]

---

[1] There is another version of the present drawing in the British Museum, which is probably a double offset; Croft-Murray & Hulton, no. 15.

Richard Wilson

(b. Penagoes 1714; d. Colommendy 1782)

90 The ruined Arch at Kew

Black, red and white chalks on blue paper.
246 × 334.

Collections:
Revd Robert Finch, by whom bequeathed
to the Taylor Institution in 1830; transferred to
the Ashmolean in 1971.

Selected literature:
Garlick, no. 57; Brown (1982), no. 1909;
Brown (1983), no. 31, Solkin, no. 99.

The present drawing is one of two known studies for a painting by Wilson executed several years after his return from Italy in 1757.[1] The painting was exhibited at the Society of Artists in 1762 with a view of the Pagoda and Palladian Bridge in Kew Gardens; the two canvases recorded the fanciful structures built as part of the beautification of the Royal Gardens carried out for George III. The ruined arch, built in 1759–60, was, according to the architect, Sir William Chambers, who was a friend of the artist, intended 'to imitate a Roman antiquity, but the structure had to serve a practical purpose as well. It was erected to make a roadway over "one of the principal walks" '. So successful was Wilson's representation of the imitation Roman ruin, the Italianate appearance of which was heightened by the artist's addition of a cedar and cypress trees depicted under a Mediterranean light and atmosphere, that until as late as 1948 the painting was thought to represent the Villa Borghese in Rome.

The effects of light and colour are brilliantly caught in this drawing. The technique seen here was one employed frequently by the artist in Italy but this is the only known instance of its use after his return to England. (After the profusion of drawings made in Italy, there are in fact few extant from the subsequent years.) It can only be supposed that the study was made to elaborate the colour scheme of the painting. The other drawing,[2] executed in chalk on white paper, is a more complete composition but differs more in detail from the painting. It may well have preceded the present study.

[1] Sir Brinsley Ford collection, London; Solkin, no. 97.
[2] Swansea; Ford, no. 71.

Thomas Gainsborough

(b. Sudbury 1727; d. London 1788)

91   Wooded Landscape with a Peasant Boy asleep in a Cart

Water- and body-colours over indications in pencil, on brown paper. 280 × 379.

Collections:

Mrs W. F. R. Weldon, by whom presented in 1934.

Selected literature:

Hayes (1970), no. 266; Brown (1982), no. 675; Hayes and Stainton, no. 30.

The drawing shows a cart with a sleeping peasant boy in the back being drawn through a rocky wooded landscape characteristic of the scenery which appears in both Gainsborough's paintings and drawings after his removal from his home town of Sudbury in Suffolk to Bath in 1759. The motif of the cart or waggon also became popular during these years and may well have been suggested to Gainsborough by his study of old master paintings in local collections, especially those of the Flemish school. The fallen log is a typical motif found in the foregrounds of paintings by Jan Wynants, who had been one of the earliest influences on the young Gainsborough. The highly finished technique can be found in other drawings by the artist of the early 1760s, and the addition of water-colour and body-colour was largely confined to works executed during this period of his life. The use of body-colour to enrich the surface may well have been suggested by the gouache drawings of Marco Ricci and Giovanni Battista Busiri, examples by both of whom were owned by a local collector and friend of Gainsborough, Robert Price; in his views of Windsor Castle of 1760, which Gainsborough may well have seen, Paul Sandby used a similar combination of water-colour and body-colour.

During his years in Bath, the artist's custom of sketching directly from nature, practised during his Suffolk years, gradually diminished in favour of imaginary studies executed in the studio. The elaborate technique developed by Gainsborough may well have been in response to his new practice of offering his drawings for sale or for presentation to friends and patrons.

Gainsborough

92 Study of a Woman seen from behind

Black chalk and stump, heightened with white on grey-green paper. 490 × 305.

Collections:

by descent through the artist's wife to Richard Lane; Sir George Donaldson; E. Buchanan; F. Lesser; E. A. Mott; Mrs Alice Jessie Mott, by whom bequeathed in memory of her husband, Charles Egerton Mott, of Oriel College, in 1959.

Selected literature:

Hayes (1970), no. 30; Garlick, no. 37; Hayes (1980), no. 19; Brown (1982), no. 673; Hayes and Stainton, no. 35.

After his move to Bath, Gainsborough painted full-length portraits as a matter of course, and to prepare himself, he made a number of large-scale chalk drawings probably studied from clothed articulated dolls, which enabled him to cope with the rich pattern of folds of female dress. The present study is similar in style and technique to this group, but unlike them, it must surely have been drawn from the life. With the motif of the dress being lifted to expose the ankle (see also the drawing by Holbein, no. 87), it is one of the most purely feminine and enchanting drawings made by the artist. Gainsborough brilliantly catches the spontaneous movement of the figure seen unusually from the back as she turns away from the artist. The mushroom hat and high heels suggest that it was drawn between 1760 and 1770.

The drawing belongs to a group of studies which the artist kept in his possession and bequeathed to his wife on his death. Although she attempted to sell as many as she could, the present sheet later passed to their younger daughter, Margaret. There is no evidence for the attractive notion, dating from the nineteenth century, that the drawing shows Gainsborough's wife on her way to church.[1]

---

[1] For a personal and evocative interpretation of the drawing, see Levey.

Francis Towne

(b. ?Exeter *c.* 1740; d. London 1816)

93 A View from the Cascade in the Groves at Ambleside

Pen and brown ink and water-colours. 377 × 265.

Signed and dated:
F. Towne delt. 1786.
Inscribed by the artist on the *verso*:
A View from the Cascade in the Grove at Ambleside the Head of the Lake of Windermere drawn on the Spot by Francis Towne August 10.th 1786 NB. The paper this is drawn on I bought myself from Rome.

Collections:
Merivale family; the Misses Merivale, by whom presented in 1922.

Selected literature:
Garlick, no. 52; Brown (1982), no. 1823; Brown (1983), no. 38.

Born in Exeter and trained in London, Towne only reached full artistic maturity during his journey in 1780–81 to Switzerland and Italy where, with his imagination responding to the scenery as a perfect embodiment of the Sublime, he developed his own highly individual style. Strong emphatic penwork was combined with sharply focussed planes of bright, rich colour, juxtaposed with one another, which produced an austerity of design and revealed the artist's love of the form and structure of the landscape.

After his return to England, his drawings became more prosaic with an obsession for topographical accuracy. But, accompanied by two friends from Exeter, Towne made a journey to the Lake District in 1786 and in the fifty or so water-colours and monochromes which resulted from the tour, he regained something of his immediate response to nature as can be seen particularly in this water-colour, one of the finest of the group. With other water-colours made on this occasion it belonged to one of his travelling companions, John Merivale, and was passed down through his family.

Drawn, as Towne makes a point of recording, on Italian laid paper brought back from Rome, which he used for several other Lake District water-colours, it catches the brilliant effect of sun breaking through the trees, and lighting up the water rushing down the cascade bordered by moss-covered boulders. He made two other drawings from the same close viewpoint, but each differs in line, light and mass, demonstrating how the artist worked up his material studied from nature in the studio to produce different effects. The Lake District, which had opened up to tourism in the late 1770s, rapidly became a source of inspiration for artists and writers in search of the Sublime and the Picturesque.

Henry Fuseli

(b. Zurich 1741; d. Putney Heath 1825)

94   Portrait of Mrs Fuseli

Water-colours over indications in pencil.
334 × 219.

Inscribed in pencil with four illegible lines of
text.

Collections:
    G. P. Dudley Wallace; Alfred Jowett, by
whom presented through the National Art-
Collections Fund in 1938.

Selected literature:
    Schiff, no. 1115; Brown (1982), no. 663;
Brown (1983), no. 45.

Fuseli, who was born in Switzerland, only settled in England in 1780, after
he had spent seven years in Italy (1770–78), where above all he fell under
the spell of Michelangelo. Following the artist's marriage to Sophia Rawlins
in 1788, he made a large number of drawings of her over the following
decade – nearly forty exist today. Not since Rubens and Rembrandt had an
artist's wife become such an important part of his art. The portraits of Mrs
Fuseli vary in character from the present study, which, although drawn in
his highly expressive style, is relatively straightforward, to representations
of his wife with fantastic costumes and hairstyles, in which the face, apart
from the staring eyes, tends to play a secondary role. Both husband and wife
had an obsessive preoccupation with hair, to pander to which Mrs Fuseli
adopted increasingly complicated and ever changing hairstyles. This unusual
type of drawing of his wife was expanded to include other highly imaginary studies of fashionable women and courtesans, which represent some of
Fuseli's most individual creations in the field of drawing. Despite the intense
erotic overtones introduced into these works by the artist, his own life, if
eccentric, was a model of respectability. The present portrait study, which
was probably drawn c. 1798, includes the same long pink gloves which his
wife is wearing in a portrait drawing dated 1790.[1]

[1] Zurich; Schiff, no. 1084.

James Barry

(b. Cork 1741; d. London 1806)

95   Portrait of the Artist

Brush in brown wash over indications in pencil on coarse brown paper. 513 × 425 (irregular).

Inscribed in pencil:
James Barry; *James Barry 1741–1806*.

Collections:
purchased in 1932 (Hope Collection).

Selected literature:
Pressly (1981), no. D63; Brown (1982), no. 330; Brown (1983), no. 43; Pressly (1983), no. 95.

During the last years of his life between 1800 and 1805, Barry made two self-portrait drawings, both of which display the same effect of strong chiaroscuro created by the heavily worked hatching done with the brush.[1] The engraver Charles Warren, who acquired the other drawing at the sale of Barry's effects in 1807, noted on the back of the sheet that 'It was a favourite candle-light study of his, but never intended to be made public'. The present study was also probably made under similar circumstances, a year or two earlier if the less gaunt appearance here is a reliable guide to dating. He is shown in the act of drawing his self-portrait; his right hand, which becomes his left in the mirror, is lightly sketched in chalk and is shown holding a pen or other instrument for drawing, and resting on the top of a table. In its uncompromisingly direct gaze, it is a powerfully honest study of the artist, without any attempt at the idealisation found in his first self-portrait. A contemporary described his appearance at the time: 'It had vulgar features, but no vulgar expression. It was rugged, austere, and passion-beaten; but the passions traced there were those of aspiring thought, and unconquerable energy, asserting itself, to the last, and sullenly exulting in its resources'.[2]

The drawing strongly conveys the disillusion and melancholy of the solitary and misunderstood genius, an accepted type of artist, who in Barry's case had also, on account of his belligerence and paranoia, made himself immensely unpopular with his fellow artists. In 1782 he had become Professor of Painting at the Royal Academy, but in 1799 he was, exceptionally, expelled on account of his controversial teaching to the students as well as for the inflammatory nature of his published writings.

[1] Royal Society of Arts, London; Pressly (1983), no. 96.
[2] Curran, p. 174.

John Robert Cozens

(b. London 1752; d. London 1797)

96   The Lake of Wallenstadt from the North-East

Water-colours over indications in pencil.
238 × 366.

Inscribed in ink on the *verso*:
    Mr. Cozens from Nature.

Collections:
    Professor F. Pierrepont Barnard, by whom bequeathed in 1934.

Selected literature:
    Brown (1982), no. 468.

Trained by his father, Alexander, who had made a number of drawings of Rome and its surroundings during his visit to Italy in 1746, John Robert left on a similar journey exactly thirty years later, passing through Switzerland in August and arriving in Rome in November 1776. He almost certainly travelled part of the time with Richard Payne Knight, the collector and influential writer on the Picturesque, who commissioned a series of Swiss views from the artist. The present water-colour, which shows the Lake of Wallensee surrounded by lofty mountains near St Gallen, can be identified from the inscription on a similar, less worked up view executed for Payne Knight: 'Glaris. Lake of Wallenstadt From the North East; The Seven Mountains'.[1] Despite the inscription on the back of the present sheet that it was done 'from Nature', it was almost cerainly worked up in the studio from an outline sketch of the kind that he frequently made on sketching trips and may very well have been done after his return to England in 1778/79.

The very limited range of colours – blues, greys and browns – producing an almost monochromatic harmony, yet at the same time achieving a marvellous richness of tone, is typical of the artist's Swiss landscapes and mark a break with conventional water-colour technique. Inspiration for these as well as their restrained colouring may well have come from William Pars's Swiss views which had been exhibited at the Royal Academy in 1771. The stormy sky hovering over the mountains produces a strain of melancholy which underlies most of Cozens's representations of what came to be regarded as the Sublime landscape of the Alps.

---

[1] Huntington Library, San Marino.

97 Sepulchral Remains in the Campagna

Water- and some body-colours over indications in pencil. 260 × 374.

Collections:
William Beckford; Henry Edridge;
Professor F. Pierrepont Barnard, by whom bequeathed in 1934.

Selected literature:
Garlick, no. 33; Brown (1982), no. 474; Sloan, p. 147.

After his return to England, John Robert Cozens became involved with William Beckford, who had been a pupil of his father. Beckford, an eccentric on the grand scale and a major figure in the Romantic movement, was a discerning collector and patron, as well as a writer. In June 1780 Cozens and Beckford set off for the Continent, travelling direct to Naples, where they arrived in early July. While Beckford continued south, Cozens had by mid-December returned to Rome, where he spent the next nine months. Although they no longer exist, he presumably filled sketch-books with studies from nature in and around Rome, in the same way that he did during the remainder of his Continental journey. These outline drawings were later worked up into enlarged water-colours, a number of which, including the present sheet, were done on commission for Beckford, probably immediately after Cozens's return home in 1783.

The scene is taken from a point on the Via Appia looking back towards Rome. The ruins in the foreground may be those of the Villa of the Quintilii, situated about four miles outside the Porta San Sebastiano. The aqueduct in the background is the Aqua Claudia, started by Caligula and completed by Claudius in 52 AD, which leads towards the Porta Maggiore. From the time that this water-colour appeared in Beckford's sale in 1805, it has been admired as one of the most lyrical and evocative studies of the light and atmosphere of the Campagna. The sense of antiquity is suggested by the rugged blocks of masonry in the foreground, the massive scale of which is indicated by the contrast with the herd of goats, those inveterate inhabitants of the landscape, seen against the skyline. The intensity of feeling expressed by this water-colour would have matched Beckford's own feelings of loneliness and isolation, recorded in his letters of the time, in one of which he described how 'a corroding melancholy preyed upon my vitals and darkened the bright sky of Italy'.

John Flaxman

(b. York 1755; d. London 1826)

98 Design for a Tomb Monument

Pen and black ink and brown wash over indications in pencil. 319 × 223.

Inscribed in pencil:
73.

Collections:
purchased in 1963.

Selected literature:
Garlick, no. 34; Brown (1982), no. 581.

The drawing shows a design for a large wall monument; in the centre three naked slaves, standing on a plinth flanked by mourners, support a circular sarcophagus. The plinth above is surmounted by a lion mask, with further decoration, including an angel in a medallion, at the top of the monument. Although one of the most splendid neo-classical sculptural designs made by the artist, there is no record of its purpose. By the mid-1780s, Flaxman was beginning to receive commissions for commemorative monuments, and after his visit to Rome from 1787 to 1794, where he was a keen student of the antique, he largely devoted himself to monumental sculpture. He was a major influence in popularising the neo-classical style in Britain. (As a result of the engravings by Tommaso Piroli after his illustrations to Dante, Homer and Æschylus, his reputation was higher on the Continent than it was in England.)

Flaxman's method as a sculptor was to make numerous drawings working out the composition and the poses of the figures, which he then transferred to plaster models, which, if needed, could be realised in marble by assistants. Like his friend George Romney, much of his creative energy was invested in drawings which were never exploited further, and it may be wondered whether he had a commission in mind when making this imposing study. It is much bolder in conception and displays a greater freedom in the application of wash when compared with the dry precise handling seen in many of his drawings.

Thomas Rowlandson

(b. London 1756; d. London 1827)

99   The Apple Vendor: 'Baking and Boiling Apples'

Pen and reddish-brown ink and water-colours over indications in pencil. 273 × 216.

Inscribed in brown ink:
Baking and Boiling Apples.

Collections:
Francis Douce, by whom bequeathed in 1834.

Selected literature:
Garlick, no. 49; Brown (1982), no. 1599.

The present drawing is a characteristic example of the artist's lively studies of daily street life, which became the material for the social satire for which he is best known. Here, a grizzled vendor is tempting various women and children of all ages with green apples from the laden paniers carried by his pony. Although it is not connected with any other known work, it is reminiscent of the series of *Cries of London* drawn by Rowlandson and issued in 1799 (only plates 1–6 and 8 are known today) and may possibly have been made with that publication in mind. There are two studies of street sellers, rather similar to the present drawing, which were later inscribed to the effect that they are unused designs for the *Cries of London*.[1]

Rowlandson, who was a very prolific draughtsman, quickly developed an expressive and highly recognisable style, which changed little during the course of his life. In many instances he started with a preliminary sketch; with this as a guide, he would lay in his composition in pencil and then work up the subject, almost invariably employing pen and ink with coloured washes to produce a tinted drawing rather than a true water-colour. Among the old masters, he had a great admiration for Rubens, reflected here in the younger women and the children, which he conveyed in an essentially rococo manner of drawing with rounded flowing lines. In his best work, he struck a fine balance between caricature and acute natural observation.

[1] Huntington Library, San Marino; Wark, nos. 101–02.

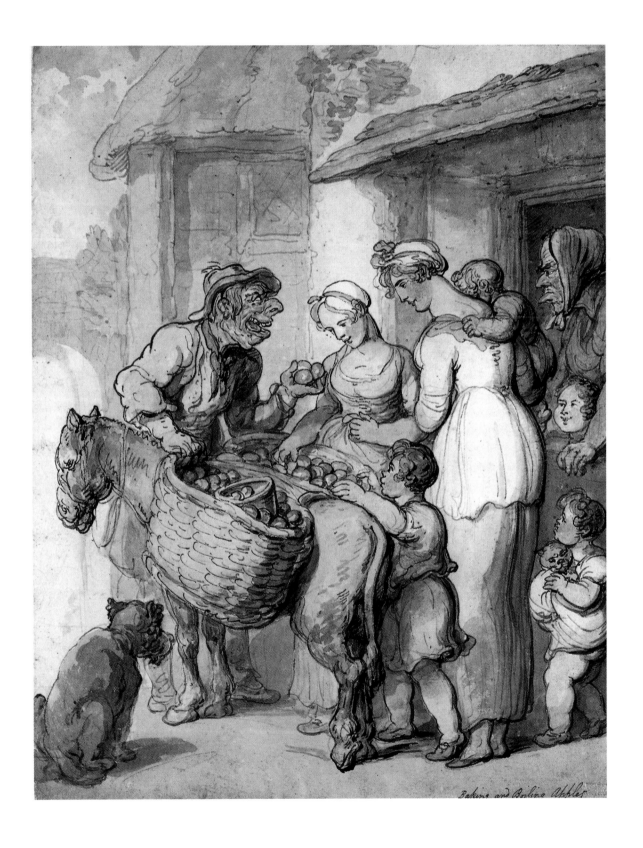

Baking and Boiling Apples

Thomas Girtin

(b. Southwark 1775; d. Southwark 1802)

100 Crowland Abbey, Lincolnshire

Water-colours over indications in pencil.
332 × 300.

Signed twice in black ink:
Girtin.

Collections:
James Moore; Miller family; Professor F. Pierrepont Barnard, by whom bequeathed in 1934.

Selected literature:
Girtin and Loshak, no. 52; Garlick, no. 40; Brown (1982), no. 708.

The present water-colour was made by Girtin on the basis of two pencil sketches by James Moore (1762–1799), one of which appears to have been completed by the former.[1] Moore, a business man and amateur artist, was a keen student of antiquity and topography, who employed professional artists to produce water-colours based on his own sketches. It has been thought that Girtin may have produced this water-colour in 1793, although it may very well date from the following year when he accompanied Moore on a tour of the Midlands, going as far north as Lincoln. (In 1794 he was also commissioned by Moore to work up the latter's Scottish drawings.) The water-colour was engraved in 1797 with the inscription that it was 'Drawn by 'I'. Girtin from a sketch by James Moore Esqr.'. The latter was published as part of Bartholomew Howlett's *Selection of Views in the County of Lincoln* in 1805, one of the many illustrated books devoted to local history which catered for the antiquarianism and taste for travel which spread throughout Britain in the late eighteenth century.

Although basing his drawing on another artist's sketch, and presumably without having seen the abbey himself, Girtin is most adept in producing a masterly example of architectural draughtsmanship, which suggests the rich and complex detail of the mediaeval building, without ever lapsing into pedantry and dryness. But this drawing remains within the eighteenth century tradition and it was only several years later that Girtin was to develop a new freedom in the use of colour and greater atmospheric fidelity, which revolutionised the technique of water-colour painting in Britain.

---

[1] Oxford; Brown (1982), nos. 1391–92.

Bibliography

Adler
  Wolfgang Adler, *Landscapes*, Corpus Rubenianum Ludwig Burchard, part XVIII, vol. I (London & Oxford, 1982)
Algarotti
  Algarotti, 'Saggio sopra l'Accademia di Francia che è in Roma', *Saggi* (Bari, 1963), 5–27
Ananoff
  Alexandre Ananoff, *L'œuvre dessiné de Jean-Honoré Fragonard (1732-1806)*, 4 vols (Paris, 1961–70)
Andrews
  Keith Andrews, *National Gallery of Scotland: Catalogue of the Italian Drawings*, 2 vols (Cambridge, 1968)
Anzelewsky
  Fedja Anzelewsky, *Albrecht Dürer: Das malerische Werk*, Jahresgabe des deutschen Vereins für Kunstwissenschaft 1970–71 (Berlin, 1971)
Bacou (1961)
  Roseline Bacou, *Dessins des Carrache* (exhib. cat., Musée du Louvre, Paris, 1961)
Bacou (1967)
  Roseline Bacou *et al.*, *Le Cabinet d'un grand amateur: P.-J. Mariette*, (exhib. cat., Musée du Louvre, Paris, 1967)
Baetjer & Links
  Katherine Baetjer & J. G. Links, *Canaletto* (exhib. cat., Metropolitan Museum of Art, New York, 1989)
Baldass
  Ludwig von Baldass, 'Notizen über holländische Zeichner des XVI Jahrhunderts, III, Jan Swart van Groningen', *Mitteilungen der Gesellschaft für vervielfältigende Kunst*, XLI (1918), 11–21
Baldinucci
  Filippo Baldinucci, *Notizie dei Professori del disegno*, 7 vols (Florence, 1974–75)
Bartsch
  Adam Bartsch, *Le Peintre graveur*, 21 vols (Vienna, 1803–21); see also *The Illustrated Bartsch* (New York, 1978–)
Bastelaer
  René van Bastelaer, *Les Estampes de Peter Bruegel l'ancien* (Brussels, 1908)
Baum
  Julius Baum, *Martin Schongauer* (Vienna, 1948)
Baumgart
  Fritz Baumgart, *Grünewald: tutti i disegni* (Florence, 1974)
Bean
  Jacob Bean, *Les Dessins italiens de la collection Bonnat* (Paris, 1960)
Benesch
  Otto Benesch, *The Drawings of Rembrandt*, 6 vols (London, 1954–57)

Bernhard
  Marianne Bernhard, *Martin Schongauer und sein Kreis: Druckgraphik, Handzeichnungen* (Munich, 1980)
Bettagno (1978)
  Alessandro Bettagno, *Disegni di Giambattista Piranesi* (exhib. cat., Fondazione Giorgio Cini, Venice, 1978)
Bettagno (1982)
  Alessandro Bettagno *et al.*, *Canaletto: Disegni – Dipinti – Incisioni* (exhib. cat., Fondazione Giorgio Cini, Venice, 1982)
Blunt & Cooke
  Anthony Blunt & Hereward Lester Cooke, *The Roman Drawings of the XVII & XVIII Centuries in the Collection of Her Majesty the Queen at Windsor Castle* (London, 1960)
Bohn
  Babette Bohn, 'The Chalk Drawings of Ludovico Carracci', *Master Drawings*, XXII (1984), 405–425
Bologna, *Guido Reni*
  Guido Reni 1575–1642 (exhib. cat., Pinacoteca Nazionale, Bologna, 1988)
Boschloo
  A. W. A. Boschloo, *Anniable Carracci in Bologna: Visible Reality in Art after the Council of Trent*, Kunsthistorische Studiën van het Nederlands Instituut te Rome, III, 2 vols (The Hague, 1974)
Boyer d'Agen
  Boyer d'Agen, *Ingres d'après une correspondance inédite* (Paris, 1909)
Briganti
  Giuliano Briganti, *Pietro da Cortona*, second edition (Florence, 1981)
Brown (1982)
  David Blayney Brown, *Ashmolean Museum Oxford: Catalogue of the Collection of Drawings*, IV, *The Earlier British Drawings* (Oxford, 1982)
Brown (1983)
  David Blayney Brown, *Early English Drawings from the Ashmolean Museum* (exhib. cat., Morton Morris & Company, London, 1983)
Buchner
  Ernst Buchner, *Das deutsche Bildnis der Spätgotik und der frühen Dürerzeit* (Berlin, 1953)
Burchard & d'Hulst
  L. Burchard & R.-A. d'Hulst, *Rubens Drawings*, 2 vols (Brussels, 1963)
Byam Shaw (1935)
  J. Byam Shaw in *The Vasari Society for the Reproduction*

of Drawings by Old and Modern Masters, second series, part XVI (1935), 5–9

Byam Shaw (1951)
J. Byam Shaw, *The Drawings of Francesco Guardi* (London, 1951)

Byam Shaw (1962)
J. Byam Shaw, *The Drawings of Domenico Tiepolo* (London, 1962)

Byam Shaw (1976)
James Byam Shaw, *Drawings by Old Masters at Christ Church Oxford*, 2 vols (Oxford, 1976)

Cailleux
Sanguines: Dessins français du dix-huitième siècle (exhib. cat., Galerie Cailleux, Paris & Geneva, 1978)

Camesasca
Ettore Camesasca, *The Complete Paintings of Watteau* (London, 1971)

Catelli Isola
Maria Catelli Isola *et al.*, *I grandi disegni italiani dal Gabinetto Nazionale delle Stampe di Roma* (Milan, n. d.)

Caylus
Comte de Caylus, 'La vie d'Antoine Watteau, peintre de figures et de paysages, sujets galants et modernes', in Edmond & Jules de Goncourt, *L'Art du dix-huitième siècle*, third edition, 2 vols (Paris, 1880–82), I, 9–32

Chiari
Maria Agnese Chiari Moretto Wiel, 'Per un catalogo ragionato dei disegni di Tiziano', *Saggi e Memorie di Storia dell'Arte*, 16 (1988), 21–99, 211–271

Cleaver
Brigid Cleaver *et al.*, *Rubens in Oxford* (exhib. cat., Christ Church, Oxford; P. & D. Colnaghi & Co. Ltd., London, 1988)

Constable & Links
W. G. Constable, *Canaletto*, second edition, revised by J. G. Links, reissued with a supplement and additional plates, 2 vols (Oxford, 1989)

Corace
Erminia Corace, ed., *Mattia Preti* (Rome, 1989)

Croft-Murray & Hulton
Edward Croft-Murray & Paul Hulton, *Catalogue of British Drawings, Volume One: XVI & XVII Centuries*, 2 vols (London, 1960)

Curran
William Henry Curran, 'Barry the Painter', *Sketches of the Irish Bar; with Essays, Literary and Political*, 2 vols (London, 1855), II, 169–183

Dacier & Vuaflart
Emile Dacier & Albert Vuaflart, *Jean de Jullienne et les graveurs de Watteau au XVIIIe siècle*, 4 vols (Paris, 1929–31)

Davies
Martin Davies, *The Earlier Italian Schools*, National Gallery Catalogues, revised edition (London, 1961)

Davis
Bruce Davis, 'The Drawings of Ciro Ferri' (doctoral dissertation, University of California, Santa Barbara, 1982)

Degrazia
Diane Degrazia, *Corregio and his Legacy: Sixteenth-Century Emilian Drawings* (exhib. cat., National Gallery of Art, Washington; Palazzo della Pilotta, Parma, 1984)

Diderot
Diderot, Salons, ed. Jean Seznec & Jean Adhémar, I, *1759, 1761, 1763*, second edition (Oxford, 1977)

Dussler
Luitpold Dussler, *Die Zeichnungen des Michelangelo: Kritischer Katalog* (Berlin, 1959)

Falk
Tilman Falk, 'Einige neugefunde Zeichnungen von Daniel Lindtmayer', *Schaffhausen Beiträge zur Geschichte*, 59 (1982), 122–135

Fischel
Oskar Fischel, *Raphaels Zeichnungen*, 8 parts (Berlin, 1913–41)

Fischel & Oberhuber
Oskar Fischel & Konrad Oberhuber, *Raphaels Zeichnungen*, part 9, *Entwürfe zu Werken Raphaels und seiner Schule im Vatican 1511/12 bis 1520* (Berlin, 1972)

Fischel (1917)
Oskar Fischel, *Die Zeichnungen der Umbrer* (Berlin, 1917)

Ford
Brinsley Ford, *The Drawings of Richard Wilson* (London, 1951)

Freedberg
S. J. Freedberg, *Andrea del Sarto*, 2 vols (Cambridge, Mass., 1963)

Friedländer
Max J. Friedländer, *Early Netherlandish Painting*, revised edition, 14 vols (Leyden & Brussels, 1967–76)

Garlick
Kenneth J. Garlick, *Eighteenth Century Master Drawings from the Ashmolean* (exhib, cat., Baltimore Museum of Art; Minneapolis Institute of Art; Kimbell Art Museum, Fort Worth; Cincinnati Art Museum, 1979–80)

Gassier
Pierre Gassier, *The Drawings of Goya*, I, *The Complete Albums* (London, 1973)

Gassier & Wilson
Pierre Gassier & Juliet Wilson, *The Life and Complete Work of Francisco Goya; with a Catalogue Raisonné of the Paintings, Drawings, and Engravings* (New York, 1971)

Gealt & Vetrocq
Adelheid M. Gealt & Marcia E. Vetrocq, *Domenico Tiepolo's Punchinello Drawings* (exhib. cat., Indiana University Art Museum; Stanford University Art Museum, 1979)

Gere
J. A. Gere, *Drawings by Raphael and his Circle from British and North American Collections* (exhib. cat., Pierpont Morgan Library, New York, 1987)

Gere & Turner (1975)
J. A. Gere & Nicholas Turner, *Drawings by Michelangelo* (exhib. cat., British Museum, London, 1975)

Gere & Turner (1983)
J. A. Gere & Nicholas Turner, *Drawings by Raphael* (exhib. cat., British Museum, London, 1983)

Girtin & Loshak
Thomas Girtin & David Loshak, *The Art of Thomas Girtin* (London, 1954)

Goossens
    Korneel Goossens, *David Vinckboons* (Antwerp & The Hague, 1954)

Grossmann
    F. Grossmann, *Bruegel, the Paintings: Complete Edition* (London, 1955)

Guillaud (1979)
    Jacqueline & Maurice Guillaud *et al.*, *Goya 1746–1828* (exhib. cat., Centre Culturel du Marais, Paris, 1979)

Guillaud (1984)
    Jacqueline & Maurice Guillaud, *Altdorfer et le réalisme fantastique dans l'art allemand* (exhib. cat., Centre Culturel du Marais, Paris, 1984)

Hagen
    Oskar Hagen, *Matthias Grünewald*, fourth edition (Munich, 1923)

Hand
    John Oliver Hand *et al.*, *The Age of Bruegel: Netherlandish Drawings in the Sixteenth Century* (exhib. cat., National Gallery of Art, Washington; Pierpont Morgan Library, New York, 1986–87)

Hartt
    Frederick Hartt, *Michelangelo Drawings* (New York, 1970)

Hayes (1970)
    John Hayes, *The Drawings of Thomas Gainsborough*, 2 vols (London, 1970)

Hayes (1980)
    John Hayes, *Thomas Gainsborough* (exhib. cat., Tate Gallery, London, 1980)

Hayes & Stainton
    John Hayes & Lindsay Stainton, *Gainsborough Drawings* (exhib. cat., International Exhibitions Foundation, Washington, 1983)

Hayward
    J. F. Hayward, *Virtuoso Goldsmiths and the Triumph of Mannerism 1540–1620* (London, 1976)

Heinemann
    Fritz Heinemann, *Giovanni Bellini e i Belliniani*, 2 vols (Venice, n. d.)

Held
    Julius S. Held, *Rubens: Selected Drawings*, second edition (Oxford, 1986)

Herrmann
    Luke Herrmann, 'The Drawings by Sir Joshua Reynolds in the Herschel Album', *Burlington Magazine*, CX (1968), 650–658

Hirst (1986)
    Michael Hirst, '*Il Modo delle Attitudini*. Michelangelo's Oxford sketchbook for the ceiling', in André Chastel *et al*, *The Sistine Chapel* (London, 1986), 208 217

Hirst (1989)
    Michael Hirst, *Michel-Ange Dessinateur* (exhib. cat., Musée du Louvre, Paris, 1989)

Hofmann (1980–81)
    Werner Hofmann *et al.*, *Goya: Das Zeitalter der Revolutionen 1789–1830* (exhib. cat., Kunsthalle, Hamburg, 1980–81)

Hollstein
    F. W. H. Hollstein, *Dutch and Flemish Engravings and Woodcuts ca. 1450–1700* (Amsterdam, 1949–)

F. W. H. Hollstein, *German Engravings, Etchings and Woodcuts ca. 1400–1700* (Amsterdam, 1954–)

Huchard & Laing
    Viviane Huchard, Alastair Laing *et al.*, *The Finest Drawings from the Museums of Angers* (exhib. cat., Heim Gallery, London, and other locations, 1977–78)

Jean-Richard
    Pierrette Jean-Richard, *L'Œuvre gravé de François Boucher dans la Collection Edmond de Rothschild* (Paris, 1978)

Joannides
    Paul Joannides, *The Drawings of Raphael with a Complete Catalogue* (Oxford, 1983)

Kahn-Rossi
    Manuela Kahn-Rossi, ed., *Pier Francesco Mola 1612–1666* (exhib. cat., Museo Cantonale d'Arte, Lugano; Musei Capitolini, Rome, 1989–90)

Kemp
    Martin Kemp *et al*, *Leonardo da Vinci* (exhib. cat. Hayward Gallery, London, 1989)

Keyes
    George S. Keyes, 'Cornelis Vroom: Marine and Landscape Artist' (doctoral dissertation, University of Utrecht, 1975)

Kitson
    Michael Kitson, *The Art of Claude Lorrain* (exhib. cat., Hayward Gallery, London, 1969)

Kloek
    Wouter Kloek, 'The Drawings of Lucas van Leyden', *Nederlands Kunsthistorisch Jaarboek*, 29 (1978), 425–458

Knox (1980)
    George Knox, *Giambattista and Domenico Tiepolo: A Study and 'Catalogue Raisonné' of the Chalk Drawings*, 2 vols (Oxford, 1980)

Knox (1983)
    George Knox *et al.*, *G. B. Piazzetta: Disegni – Incisioni – Libri – Manoscritti* (exhib. cat., Fondazione Giorgio Cini, Venice, 1983)

Koegler
    Hans Koegler, *Beschreibendes Verzeichnis des Basler Handzeichnungen des Urs Graf, nebst einem Katalog der Basler Urs Graf-Ausstellung* (Basel, 1926)

Kruft
    Hanno-Walter Kruft 'Ein Album mit Porträtzeichnungen Ottavio Leonis', *Storia dell'Arte*, IV (1969), 447–458

L.
    Frits Lugt, *Les Marques de collections de dessins et d'estampes* (Amsterdam, 1921) and *Supplément* (The Hague, 1956)

La Font de Saint Yenne
    La Font de Saint Yenne, *Réflexions sur quelques causes de l'état présent de la peinture en France. Avec un examen des principaux ouvrages exposés au Louvre le mois d'Août 1746* (The Hague, 1747)

Langedijk
    Karla Langedijk, *The Portraits of the Medici, 15th–18th Centuries*, 3 vols (Florence, 1981–87)

Lapauze
    Henry Lapauze, *Ingres: Sa vie & son oeuvre (1780–1867) d'après des documents inédits* (Paris, 1911)

Lauts

Jan Lauts, *Carpaccio: Paintings and Drawings* (London, 1962)

Le Blanc

Charles Le Blanc, *Manuel de l'amateur d'estampes*, 4 vols (Paris, 1854–90)

Levey

Michael Levey, 'Thomas Gainsborough: Drawing of a Woman seen from Back', *The Ashmolean*, No. 15 (Spring, 1989), 9–11

Lloyd (1977)

Christopher Lloyd, *A Catalogue of the Earlier Italian Paintings in the Ashmolean Museum* (Oxford, 1977)

Lloyd (1982)

Christopher Lloyd, *Dürer to Cézanne: Northern European Drawings from the Ashmolean Museum* (exhib. cat., Jane Voorhees Zimmerli Art Museum, Rutgers University, New Brunswick; Cleveland Museum of Art, 1982–83)

Lo Bianco

Anna Lo Bianco, *Pier Leone Ghezzi Pittore* (Palermo, 1985)

Macandrew

Hugh Macandrew, *Ashmolean Museum, Oxford: Catalogue of the Collection of Drawings*, III, *Italian Schools: Supplement* (Oxford, 1980)

Mahon

Denis Mahon, *Mostra dei Carracci* (exhib. cat., Palazzo dell'Archiginnasio, Bologna, second edition, 1963)

Mariuz

Adriano Mariuz, *L'opera completa del Piazzetta* (Milan, 1982)

Meij

A. W. F. M. Meij *et al.*, *Jacques de Gheyn II 1565–1629: Drawings* (exhib. cat., Museum Boymans-van Beuningen, Rotterdam; National Gallery of Art, Washington, 1985–86)

Mielke

Hans Mielke, *Albrecht Altdorfer: Zeichnungen, Deckfarben- malerei, Druckgraphik* (exhib. cat., Kupferstichkabinett, Berlin; Staatliche Museen Preussischer Kulturbesitz, Berlin; Museen der Stadt Regensburg, 1988)

Millar (1963)

Oliver Millar, *The Tudor, Stuart and Early Georgian Pictures in the Collection of Her Majesty the Queen*, 2 vols (London, 1963)

Millar (1978)

Oliver Millar, *Sir Peter Lely 1618–80* (exhib. cat., National Portrait Gallery, London, 1978)

Monbeig Goguel

Catherine Monbeig Goguel, 'Un tableau d'autel de Cristofano Gherardi à Recanati', *Paragone*, XXVIII, no. 327 (May 1977), 108–116

Monducci & Pirondini

Elio Monducci & Massimo Pirondini, *Lelio Orsi* (exhib. cat., Teatro Valli, Reggio Emilia, 1987–88)

Morassi, *Dipinti*

Antonio Morassi, *Guardi: I dipinti*, 2 vols (Venice, 1984)

Morassi, *Disegni*

Antonio Morassi, *Guardi: I disegni* (Venice, 1973)

Morassi (1962)

Antonio Morassi, *A Complete Catalogue of the Paintings of G. B. Tiepolo* (London, 1962)

Münz

Ludwig Münz, *Bruegel, The Drawings: Complete Edition* (London, 1961)

Munhall

Edgar Munhall, *Jean-Baptiste Greuze 1725–1805* (exhib. cat., Wadsworth Atheneum, Hartford, and other locations, 1976–77)

Muraro

Michelangelo Muraro, *I disegni di Vittore Carpaccio*, Corpus Graphicum, 2 (Florence, 1977)

Naef

Hans Naef, *Die Bildniszeichnungen von J.-A.-D. Ingres*, 5 vols (Bern, 1977)

Olszewski

Edward J. Olszewski, *The Draftsman's Eye: Late Italian Renaissance Schools and Styles* (exhib. cat., Cleveland Museum of Art, 1981)

Opperman (1966)

H. N. Opperman, 'Some animal drawings by Jean- Baptiste Oudry', *Master Drawings*, IV (1966), 384–409

Opperman (1977)

H. N. Opperman, *Jean-Baptiste Oudry*, 2 vols (New York & London, 1977)

Ostrow

Stephen E. Ostrow, 'A Drawing by Annibale Carracci for the Jason Frescoes and the S. Gregorio "Baptism"', *Master Drawings*, VIII (1970), 40–42

Panofsky

Erwin Panofsky, *Albrecht Dürer*, second edition, 2 vols (Princeton, 1945)

Parker, I

K. T. Parker, *Catalogue of the Collection of Drawings in the Ashmolean Museum*, I, *Netherlandish, German, French and Spanish Schools*, (Oxford, 1938)

Parker, II

K. T. Parker, *Catalogue of the Collection of Drawings in the Ashmolean Museum*, II, *Italian Schools*, (Oxford, 1956)

Parker (1952)

K. T. Parker, in *Ashmolean Museum: Report of the Visitors 1952*

Parker (1958)

K. T. Parker, *Disegni veneti di Oxford*, (exhib. cat., Fondazione Giorgio Cini, Venice, 1958)

Parker & Mathey

K. T. Parker & J. Mathey, *Antoine Watteau: Catalogue complet de son oeuvre dessiné*, 2 vols (Paris, 1957)

Pérez Sánchez

Alfonso E. Pérez Sánchez *et al.*, *Goya and the Spirit of Enlightenment* (exhib. cat., Museo del Prado, Madrid; Museum of Fine Arts, Boston; Metropolitan Museum of Art, New York, 1988–89)

Pignatti (1963)

Terisio Pignatti, Review of Jan Lauts, *Carpaccio: Paintings and Drawings, Master Drawings*, I, no. 4 (1963), 47–53

Pignatti (1969)

Terisio Pignatti, '"Sei Villaggi Campestri" dal Canaletto', *Bollettino dei Musei Civici Veneziani*, XIV, no. 3 (1969), 23–28

Pignatti (1977)

Terisio Pignatti, *Italian Drawings in Oxford from the Collections of the Ashmolean Museum and Christ Church* (Oxford, 1977)

Pignatti (1981)

Terisio Pignatti, ed., *Le Scuole di Venezia* (Milan, 1981)

Pizzorusso

Claudio Pizzorusso, *Ricerche su Cristofano Allori*, Accademia Toscana di Scienze e Lettere 'La Colombaria', Studi, LX (Florence, 1982)

Popham (1928)

A. E. Popham, 'Notes on Flemish domestic Glass Painting', *Apollo*, VII (1928), 175–179.

Popham (1931)

A. E. Popham, 'Die Josefs Legende', *Berliner Museen*, LII (1931), 73–76, 122.

Popham (1946)

A. E. Popham, *The Drawings of Leonardo da Vinci* (London, 1946)

Popham (1967)

A. E. Popham, *Italian Drawings in the Department of Prints and Drawings in the British Museum: Artists working in Parma in the Sixteenth Century*, 2 vols (London, 1967)

Popham (1971)

A. E. Popham, *Catalogue of the Drawings of Parmigianino*, 3 vols (New Haven & London, 1971)

Popham & Pouncey

A. E. Popham & Philip Pouncey, *Italian Drawings in the Department of Prints and Drawings in the British Museum: The Fourteenth and Fifteenth Centuries*, 2 vols (London, 1950)

Popham & Wilde

A. E. Popham & J. Wilde, *The Italian Drawings of the XV and XVI Centuries in the Collection of His Majesty the King at Windsor Castle* (London, 1949)

Posner

Donald Posner, *Annibale Carracci: a Study in the Reform of Italian Painting around 1590*, 2 vols (London, 1971)

Pressly (1981)

William L. Pressly, *The Life and Art of James Barry* (New Haven & London, 1981)

Pressly (1983)

William L. Pressly, *James Barry: The Artist as Hero* (exhib. cat., Tate Gallery, London, 1983)

Prouté (1986)

Catalogue 'Tintoretto': Dessins, Estampes . . . en vente chez Paul Prouté S.A. (Paris, 1986)

Prouté (1988)

Catalogue 'Millet': Dessins, Estampes . . . en vente chez Paul Prouté S.A. (Paris, 1988)

Reznicek

E. K. J. Reznicek, *Die Zeichnungen von Hendrick Goltzius Mit einem beschreibenden Katalog*, 2 vols (Utrecht, 1961)

Ridolfi

Carlo Ridolfi, *Le Meraviglie dell'arte*, ed. Detlev von Hadeln, 2 vols (Berlin, 1914–24)

Robertson

Giles Robertson, *Giovanni Bellini* (Oxford, 1968)

Roethlisberger (1961)

Marcel Roethlisberger, *Claude Lorrain: The Paintings*, 2 vols (New Haven, 1961)

Roethlisberger (1968)

Marcel Roethlisberger, *Claude Lorrain: The Drawings*, 2 vols (Berkeley & Los Angeles, 1968)

Romani

Vittoria Romani, 'Lelio Orsi e Roma: fra maniera raffaellesca e maniera michelangiolesca', *Prospettiva*, 29 (1982), 41–61

Rosenberg

Pierre Rosenberg, *Fragonard* (exhib. cat., Grand Palais, Paris; Metropolitan Museum of Art, New York, 1987–88)

Rossi

Paola Rossi, *I disegni di Jacopo Tintoretto*, Corpus Graphicum, 1 (Florence, 1975)

Rothschild

Kate de Rothschild & Yvonne Tan Bunzl, *Master Drawings* (London, 1990)

Rowlands

John Rowlands, *The Age of Dürer and Holbein* (exhib. cat., British Museum, London, 1988)

Ruhmer

Eberhard Ruhmer, *Grünewald Drawings: Complete Edition* (London, 1970)

Salamon

Ferdinando Salamon, *G. B. Piranesi: acquaforti e disegni* (exhib. cat., Galleria Civica d'Arte Moderna, Turin, 1961–2)

Scarpellini

Pietro Scarpellini, *Perugino* (Milan, 1984)

Schiff

Gert Schiff, *Johann Heinrich Füssli* 1741–1825, Oeuvrekataloge Schweizer Künstler, I, 2 vols (Zürich & Munich, 1973)

Schneider

Cynthia P. Schneider, *Rembrandt's Landscapes: Drawings and Prints* (exhib. cat., National Gallery of Art, Washington, 1990)

Schwarz

Heinrich Schwarz, 'Palma Giovane and his Family: Observations on some Portrait Drawings', *Master Drawings*, III (1965), 158–165

Shearman

John Shearman, *Andrea del Sarto*, 2 vols (Oxford, 1965)

Sloan

Kim Sloan, *Alexander and John Robert Cozens: The Poetry of Landscape* (New Haven & London, 1986)

Solkin

David H. Solkin, *Richard Wilson: The Landscape of Reaction* (exhib. cat., Tate Gallery, London, 1982–83)

Spike

John T. Spike, 'Ottavio Leoni's Portraits *alla macchia*', in *Baroque Portraits in Italy: Works from North American Collections* (exhib. cat., John and Mable Ringling Museum, Sarasota; Wadsworth Atheneum, Hartford, 1984–85)

Stainton & White

Lindsay Stainton & Christopher White, *Drawing in England from Hilliard to Hogarth* (exhib. cat., British Museum, London, 1987)

Sumowski, *Drawings*
Werner Sumowski, *Drawings of the Rembrandt School* (New York, 1979–)

Sumowski, *Gemälde*
Werner Sumowski, *Gemälde der Rembrandt Schüle*, 4 vols (Landau, 1983)

Sutherland Harris
Ann Sutherland Harris, *Selected Drawings of Gian Lorenzo Bernini* (New York, 1977)

Sutton
Denys Sutton, *Italian Drawings from the Ashmolean Museum, Oxford* (exhib. cat., Wildenstein & Co. Ltd., London, 1970)

Tempestini
Anchise Tempestini, *Martino da Udine detto Pellegrino da San Daniele* (Udine, 1979)

Testori & Bianconi
G. Testori & P. Bianconi, *L'Opera completa di Grünewald* (Milan, 1972)

Thomas
Hylton Thomas, *The Drawings of Giovanni Battista Piranesi* (London, 1954)

Thuillier & Montagu
Jacques Thuillier & Jennifer Montagu, *Charles Le Brun 1619–1690: Peintre et Dessinateur* (exhib. cat., Château de Versailles, 1963)

Tolnay
Charles de Tolnay, *Corpus dei disegni di Michelangelo*, 4 vols (Novara, 1975–80)

Turner
Nicholas Turner, *Florentine Drawings of the Sixteenth Century* (exhib. cat., British Museum, London, 1986)

Van Puyvelde
Leo van Puyvelde, *The Flemish Drawings in the Collection of His Majesty the King at Windsor Castle* (London, 1942)

Van Regteren Altena (1967)
J. Q. van Regteren Altena, 'The origin of a motif in Rembrandt's work', *Master Drawings*, V (1967), 375–378

Van Regteren Altena (1983)
I. Q. van Regteren Altena, *Jacques de Gheyn: Three Generations*, 3 vols (The Hague, Boston, London, 1983)

Venice, *Tiziano*
Tiziano (exhib. cat., Palazzo Ducale, Venice, 1990)

Vos
Rik Vos, *Lucas van Leyden* (Bentveld & Maarssen, 1978)

Wagner
Hugo Wagner *et al.*, *Niklaus Manuel Deutsch: Maler, Dichter, Staatsmann* (exhib. cat., Kunstmuseum, Bern, 1979)

Wark
Robert R. Wark, *Drawings by Thomas Rowlandson in the Huntington Collection* (San Marino, 1975)

Washington, *The Age of Correggio and the Carracci*
The Age of Correggio and the Carracci: Emilian Painting of the Sixteenth and Seventeenth Centuries (exhib. cat., National Gallery of Art, Washington, and other locations, 1986–87)

Wessely
J. E. Wessely, *Antonj Waterloo: Verzeichniss seiner Radirten Blätter* (Hamburg, 1891)

Wethey (1975)
Harold E. Wethey, *The Paintings of Titian: Complete Edition*, III, *The Mythological and Historical Paintings* (London, 1975)

Wethey (1987)
Harold E. Wethey, *Titian and his Drawings* (Princeton, 1987)

White
Christopher White, *The Dutch Pictures in the Collection of Her Majesty the Queen* (Cambridge, 1982)

Wilde
Johannes Wilde, *Italian Drawings in the Department of Prints and Drawings in the British Museum: Michelangelo and his Studio,* (London, 1953)

Wilton-Ely
John Wilton-Ely, *Piranesi* (exhib. cat., Arts Council of Great Britain, London, 1978)

Winkler
Friedrich Winkler, *Die Zeichnungen Albrecht Dürers*, 4 vols (Berlin, 1936–39)

Winner (1961)
Matthias Winner, 'Zeichnungen des älteren Jan Brueghel', *Jahrbuch der Berliner Museen*, III (1961), 190–241

Winner (1975)
Matthias Winner et al., *Pieter Bruegel d. Ä. als Zeichner: Herkunft und Nachfolge* (exhib. cat., Staatliche Museen Preussischer Kulturbesitz, Berlin, 1975)

Winzinger
Franz Winzinger, *Albrecht Altdorfer Zeichnungen* (Munich, 1952)

Wittkower
R. Wittkower, 'Works by Bernini at the Royal Academy', *Burlington Magazine*, XCIII (1951), 51–56

Index of artists